GO FOR

Physical Education Activities for the Classroom Teacher

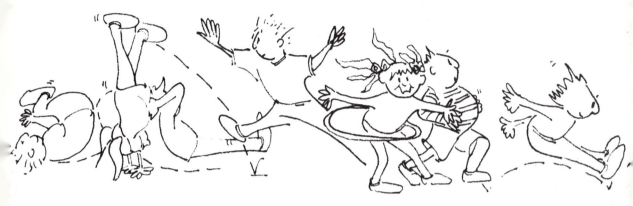

CATHERINE ROBERTS

OXFORD
UNIVERSITY PRESS

Melbourne

OXFORD UNIVERSITY PRESS AUSTRALIA

Oxford New York Toronto
Delhi Bombay Calcutta Madras Karachi
Petaling Jaya Singapore Hong Kong Tokyo
Nairobi Dar es Salaam Cape Town
Melbourne Auckland
and associated companies in
Berlin Ibadan

OXFORD is a trademark of Oxford University Press

First published 1987
Reprinted 1987 (twice), 1989, 1990

National Library of Australia
Cataloguing-in-Publication data:

Roberts, Catherine
 Go for It!: physical education activities for the classroom teacher.

 ISBN 0 19 554654 7.

 1. Physical education for children. I. Title.

372.8'6044

Design and illustrations by Karen Hopkins
Typeset by Post Typesetting, Brisbane
Printed in Hong Kong
Published by Oxford University Press,
253 Normanby Road, South Melbourne

D. Haigh

CONTENTS

INTRODUCTION

The program of activities in this book comprises a set of sequential lessons for the school year, covering the major areas of physical education — ball handling, gymnastics, athletics, fitness, minor and major games, and movement awareness. The book is divided into three sections appropriate to three age groups — Prep to Grade 2, Grades 3 and 4, and Grades 5 and 6. Each section is made up of three units, each unit being divided into six lessons, covering four activities, thus making a total of 72 lessons in each section.

The program's focus is on primary education, but it may well be very relevant to post-primary settings, particularly the early post-primary years and remedial physical education.

The need for regular physical activity was fulfilled in the past as the lifestyle demanded physical effort; but present day society demands much less. As a result our lungs are not used fully, nor is the heart sufficiently stimulated to produce a training effect. Also, the nature of schooling, where the majority of time is spent sitting at a desk, requires that children be involved in some form of daily activity. This planned introduction to skills, experiences and training in attitudes is vital to provide the children with stimulation, variety and increased concentration in the school day.

The non-competitive approach to daily activity allows for differences in individual skill levels; participation is the essence. This program provides a planned, systematic framework where daily activity is a scheduled event of every day, as recommended by the National Heart Foundation. It is designed so that no special organization is required, and it can be taken by a specialist physical education teacher or by the classroom teacher, individually, or in a platoon arrangement. It can even fit in a rural school routine.

A platoon arrangement involves a group of grades having a set time on particular days to participate in the different areas of P.E. together. The program allows for a minimum of two weeks to be spent on each area. Extra time can also be allowed for reviewing lessons. The teachers can follow their group to the different areas of P.E. or be responsible for one particular area and take the other grades for these lessons also.

The following organization involves four grades (3A, 3B, 4A, 4B) spending two weeks on each area.

WEEKS

Week	1	2	3	4	5	6	7	8
Gymnastics	3A	3A	4B	4B	4A	4A	3B	3B
Ball handling	3B	3B	3A	3A	4B	4B	4A	4A
Athletics	4A	4A	3B	3B	3A	3A	4B	4B
Minor games/ fitness	4B	4B	4A	4A	3B	3B	3A	3A

An added feature is the inclusion of classroom related activities. These are related to the various physical education areas to enable the classroom teacher to integrate physical education into the classroom.

Since this is a book for the classroom teacher, activities requiring specialized knowledge or extensive organization have been omitted.

Instructions and diagrams are simple and easy to follow, and the two symbols used throughout denote 'teaching points' **(T)** and 'demonstrations' **(D)** suggesting to the teacher that certain points should be stressed or that demonstrations would be useful.

This is a practical, tested set of sequential lesson plans — *Go For It!*

A CHECKLIST FOR A WORTHWHILE P.E. PROGRAM

Physical Skills and Fitness
Prep-Grade 2
- develop the infants' natural tendency to play and explore
- maintain their physical vitality
- assist normal growth and development patterns
- develop confidence and experiences in movement and coordination.

Grade 3/4
- develop body control
- assist normal growth and development
- develop natural levels of fitness
- develop basic ball handling skills.

Grade 5/6
- be competent and confident in basic movement and coordination
- apply skills in a cooperative and competitive way
- extend basic ball handling skills
- develop ways to improve and maintain fitness
- encourage lifestyles that include regular activity.

Knowledge and Understanding
Prep-Grade 2
- to be aware of what the body can do — use movement to understand concepts related to other areas of the curriculum.

Grade 3/4
- be aware of a healthy body
- be aware of leisure time activities
- understand the importance of physical activity
- develop respect for rules and umpires.

Grade 5/6
- develop leisure time activities
- be aware of different activities in the community
- acquire knowledge and skills needed to follow a healthy lifestyle
- understand the importance of physical fitness
- understand responsibilities when involved in competition.

Attitude and Appreciation
Prep-Grade 2
- are the children enjoying P. E.?
- are they happy, healthy and energetic?
- are they keen to demonstrate their skills?
- are they able to play cooperatively in small groups?

Grade 3/4
- are they willing to try new skills?
- are they keen to demonstrate their skills?
- are they aware of team involvement?
- are they cooperative in small groups and team situations?
- are they aware of their individual performance?

Grade 5/6
- do the children have a positive attitude to and enjoy physical activity?
- do they have confidence in small or large groups?
- do they show initiative in developing ideas?
- are they willing to try new challenges?
- do they respect the rules of games and codes of behaviour?

PREP~GRADE 2
Gymnastics

The children will experience basic movement concepts of running, jumping, shapes, balances.

Helpful hints
□ Encourage the children to think of different shapes (do not be the same as the person next to you).
□ Use demonstration to stimulate different ideas, and to help maintain concentration.
□ Make sure you have everyone's full attention when a demonstration is taking place.
□ Ensure that both the children and yourself are enjoying the physical activity.

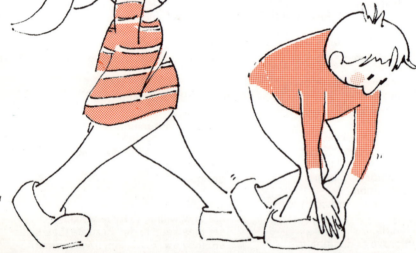

RELATED CLASSROOM ACTIVITIES
Major theme — animals
□ Discuss and make a list of animals that can make themselves into a **curled shape**, e.g. snail, cat, dog, kangaroo, lion.
□ Discuss and make a list of animals that can **stretch** up high, e.g. bear, monkey, kangaroo.
□ When do you stretch up high? e.g. to catch a high ball, to reach something, to look over a crowd, to look over a fence.
□ Discuss and make a list of animals that can **jump**, e.g. frog, bird, kangaroo.
□ How many **body supports** do you have when standing? e.g. two feet.

□ How many body supports do different animals have? e.g. bird, dog, cat, tiger, octopus, elephant.
□ What things do you do that need **balance**? e.g. standing, sitting, walking, bike-riding, ice-skating, kicking a ball.

These activities are intended to help the children relate the concepts of various movements to things, in this case animals, with which they are familiar.

LESSON 1

Equipment
A beanbag each.

Warm-up
Move around the area in different ways, e.g. walk, jump, hop, skip.
Run and jump in the air to touch the sun.

Skills
Standing in a space by yourself:
- Make yourself into the shape of a ball.
- Make yourself into a curled shape.
- Move around in a curled shape like a mouse.
- Jump around; on the whistle, stop and make yourself into a curled shape.
- See how tall you can make yourself.
- What are you doing with your arms? Introduce the concept of stretching.
- Run around stretching as much as you can, on the whistle, make yourself into a curled shape.
- Ⓓ Try and make yourself as wide as a river.

Application
- With a beanbag on your back, make a curled shape.
- Make a curled shape with your nose on the beanbag.
- Run and jump over your beanbag, make a curled/wide shape.
- What shape am I? (Children guess what shape is being made by another person, e.g. wide shape on feet and hands.)

LESSON 2

Equipment
A hoop each. One long skipping rope.

Warm-up
Run away from me and on the whistle jump back to me. Variation — hop, walk, skip.
Action rhyme: I can clap high,
                 I can clap low,
                 I jump jump jump,
                 And down I go.
This rhyme can be repeated at different speeds.

Skills
- Select a child to make a curled shape. Everybody tries to make the same curled shape.
- Try and move in that shape.
- See if you can make a different shape when you jump.
- Teacher shows a twisted rope. Everyone tries to twist like the rope. Twist fingers, hands, arms, legs, feet.

Application
Everyone has a hoop:
- Try and make a curled shape inside your hoop.
- Make a different curled shape inside your hoop.
- Make any shape inside your hoop.   Ⓓ
- Jump out of your hoop and make a shape.
- Run around and on the whistle use any hoop to make a wide shape.
- Repeat using different shapes.

LESSON 3

Equipment
A hoop each.

Warm-up
Be a plane flying around, do not crash into anyone else. On the whistle, land on the ground. Bend and touch your toes — say hello to them. Shake various body parts — fingers, hands, feet, head.

Skills
- Run around and on the whistle, make a wide shape.
- 'Look at John, he is using his feet as body supports'.
- Explain term 'body supports', i.e. parts of the body in contact with the ground.
- Count the number of body supports you use.
- Make a curled shape using your back as a body support.
- Make any shape using two feet and two hands as body supports.
- Move around in this shape.
- Jump like a kangaroo. How many body supports does a kangaroo use?
- Move around using one body support.
- Vary the movements using two, three or four body supports.

Application
- Free play with hoop. Select a child who may be skipping, jumping or running with hoop. How many body supports are being used?

All try to do it.
- ☐ Place hoop on ground. Move around hoop on two body supports.
- ☐ Move over hoop on two body supports.
- ☐ Make a wide shape on four body supports using your hoop.

LESSON 4

Equipment
A beanbag each.

Warm-up
Pretend you are driving a car, move as fast as you can. Be careful not to crash.
Ⓓ Move like something that goes up in the air.

Skills
- ☐ Run around the area, on the whistle make a curled shape.
- ☐ Point out various body supports.
- ☐ Make a curled shape using your back as a body support.
- ☐ See if you can move on your back (rocking).
- ☐ Move around the area on one body support. What action is this?
- ☐ Move around the area on two body supports, e.g. hand and foot.
- ☐ Repeat above using a different number of body supports and different shapes.

Application
In the following activities it is important to encourage and discuss a variety of shapes and body supports.
Ⓓ ☐ Place your beanbag on your head and make a stretched shape on one and two body supports. Move around in this shape.
- ☐ With beanbag on back, make a wide shape using four body supports.
- ☐ Repeat with beanbag on stomach and using three body supports.
- ☐ Place beanbag on ground and move around it on three body supports.
- ☐ Move over the beanbag on three body supports.
- ☐ Repeat above using one and two body supports.

LESSON 5

Equipment
A beanbag and a hoop each.

Warm-up
Move around like an elephant. Variations — duck, crab, snake, tiger.
Children stand around the teacher:
   'Run to the tree and back to me.'
   'Run to the seat and back to me.'
In your own space stretch various body parts.

Skills
- ☐ Introduce the term **balance**, i.e. a still position like a statue.
- ☐ Children make a shape and hold it still   Ⓓ
- ☐ Make a curled balance. Variations — wide, twisted.

Question the body shape and body supports   Ⓣ
used.
- ☐ Make a balance using a beanbag or a hoop, e.g. a curled balance inside a hoop.
- ☐ Repeat above making a different balance.
- ☐ Run around with a beanbag or a hoop, on the whistle, stop and make a wide balance.
- ☐ Repeat several times with variations so that the children change smoothly from one activity to the next, e.g. run — balance — run — balance.

Allow time for demonstration and discussion of   Ⓣ
the different body supports used in the balance.

Application
Game, 'Freeze'. Teacher stands with back to the class. Children move around on one, two or three body supports. On the whistle they freeze and the teacher looks for anyone who may still be moving.

LESSON 6

Equipment
Adventure playground or seats in school yard.

Warm-up
Jump around like a kangaroo.
Pretend you are a bouncing ball, jumping from high to low bounces.
Pretend you have a ball and kick it as far as you can, then throw it, roll it, hit it.

Skills

- ☐ In your own space make a balance in a wide shape using four body supports.
- ☐ Make a different wide shape with two body supports.
- ☐ Move around the area on four body supports, on the whistle, balance on two body supports.
- ☐ Move around the area on two body supports, on the whistle, balance on four body supports.
- ☐ Repeat above with different body supports.

Ⓣ Encourage variety in movement and shapes.

Application

- ☐ Jump off equipment making different shapes. Bend knees on landing.
- ☐ How many body supports do you use to land?

Ⓓ ☐ Balancing on equipment or seats: make a wide balance. Make a wide balance with your hands and feet as body support. Make a curled balance with your back as body support. Make a different balance using other parts of your body.

Ⓣ Encourage variety in shapes.

PREP~GRADE 2
Ball Handling

The children will experience hitting, rolling, bouncing, dribbling, throwing, catching, using beanbags and balls

Helpful hints

- Distribute equipment to children standing in lines.
- It is best for the teacher to hand out equipment.
- A good way to get the children into pairs — 'Find yourself a partner and bob down quickly'.
- On the whistle, children should immediately stop and place ball/beanbag between their feet.
- Give positive reinforcement to those who stop immediately on the whistle, it encourages the rest of the class.
- Always give demonstrations in a lesson and insist that everyone is watching.

RELATED CLASSROOM ACTIVITIES
Major theme — games

- Discuss and make a list of things that roll, e.g. hoop, tyre, ball, can etc.
- Add to the list of 'rolling' games, e.g. ten pin bowling, soccer, softball.
- Make a list of bouncing games, e.g. tennis, bat-tennis, table-tennis.
- Make a list of hitting games, e.g. softball, cricket, tennis, baseball.

- Which games include throwing and catching? e.g. basketball, netball, softball, cricket.

These activities will help to demonstrate the value of ball handling skills.

LESSON 1

Equipment
A beanbag each.

Warm-up
Move around the area with the beanbag doing whatever you like. On the whistle, stop, place beanbag between feet. See who stops first.

Skills
(D) □ Move the beanbag in different ways, e.g. throwing, hitting, balancing.
□ Use different parts of your body to move the beanbag.
□ Count the number of body parts you can use.
□ Move around the area keeping the beanbag close to the ground, e.g. kicking, rolling, balancing on toes.
□ Use a different body part to keep the beanbag close to the ground.
□ Throw the beanbag up. Keep it off the ground.
□ What other parts of your body can put the beanbag in the air?

Application
□ Relay: balancing beanbag on head, walk up to line and back.
□ Variation — walk sideways or backwards.

LESSON 2

Equipment
A beanbag each.

Warm-up
Staying on the spot, run quickly. When teacher claps hands, run anywhere within the boundary. Repeat with variations, e.g. hopping, jumping, skipping.

Skills
□ Move the beanbag in different ways while standing on the spot.
(D) □ Use a different body part.
□ See what you can do with your beanbag while moving about the area.
□ Use different body parts.
□ Throw the beanbag into the air. Can you catch it?

Stress the importance of watching the beanbag. (T)
Reach up to meet the beanbag before it hits the ground.
Move around the area as you throw the beanbag up.

Application
□ Relay. Walk up to the line and back throwing up and catching the beanbag.
□ Variations: repeat the relay running, skipping, walking sideways or walking backwards.

LESSON 3

Equipment
A beanbag each.

Warm-up
Move around like a train/butterfly/motorbike/bird/car/rabbit.

Skills
□ Practise throwing the beanbag into the air and catching it before it hits the ground.
□ Stress keeping eyes on the beanbag, and (T) moving to catch it.
□ Walk around the area, throwing and catching the beanbag.
□ Gradually move faster as you throw and catch the beanbag.
□ With a partner standing 1 metre apart, throw and catch the beanbag, sit on the ground and throw the beanbag to each other; throw and catch using two hands, then one hand.

Application
□ With a partner, throw and catch beanbag ten times, while sitting, then while standing.

LESSON 4

Equipment
A ball each.

Warm-up
Select someone to stand at the front of the class. Everyone asks, 'What did you see on your way to school?' Child gives various replies, e.g. dog, car, bird, kangaroo. The children then move around like the object of the reply.

11

Skills

(D) □ Find the different things you can do with the ball. Keep it **close** to you.

(D) □ Try using different parts of your body to move the ball, e.g. knee, elbow, nose, finger, head.

□ On 'change' use another body part to move the ball.

□ Move the ball keeping it close to the ground.

(D) □ Use different body parts keeping the ball close to the ground.

□ In pairs, standing 1 metre apart, pass the ball keeping it close to the ground. Then pass the ball using different body parts, keeping it close to the ground.

Application

□ In pairs roll ball to each other ten times while standing, then sitting.

□ Variations: increase the distance, use different body parts.

LESSON 5

Equipment
A ball each.

Warm-up
Move around the area like a bouncing ball.
Move around like a spinning ball.
Run around area, on 'stop' change to a squat position, on 'go' run around.

Skills

□ Move the ball in various ways, following it closely.

□ Move the ball close to the ground using different body parts, e.g. rolling, low bouncing.

□ Move the ball without moving off your spot.

□ Find different ways of moving the ball on the spot.

□ Use your favourite way to move the ball about the area.

□ Use your favourite way to move the ball on the spot.

(D) □ Join the above two ways to make a sequence.

Application

□ 'Keep the bucket full': teacher throws out balls as quickly as possible. Children run and collect the balls and bring back to the container. They can only collect one ball at a time.

LESSON 6

Equipment
A ball each.

Warm-up
'Keep the bucket full', as in Lesson 5.

Skills

□ Find different ways of moving the ball close to your feet, using your **feet**.

Give demonstrations, e.g. kick, dribble, jump. (D)

□ Move the ball with your feet along the ground.

□ See how many ways you move the ball using your hands.

□ Keep the ball off the ground using your hands.

Give demonstrations, e.g. throwing, catching, (D) pushing in air, balancing.

□ Begin by using your **hands**. On 'change' use your **feet**.

Application

□ With a partner, pass the ball using different parts of your **feet**.

□ Try to pass the ball straight to your partner.

□ See how many different ways you can pass the ball using your **hands**.

□ Pass the ball using your **hands**, then using your **feet**.

PREP~GRADE 2
Movement Awareness

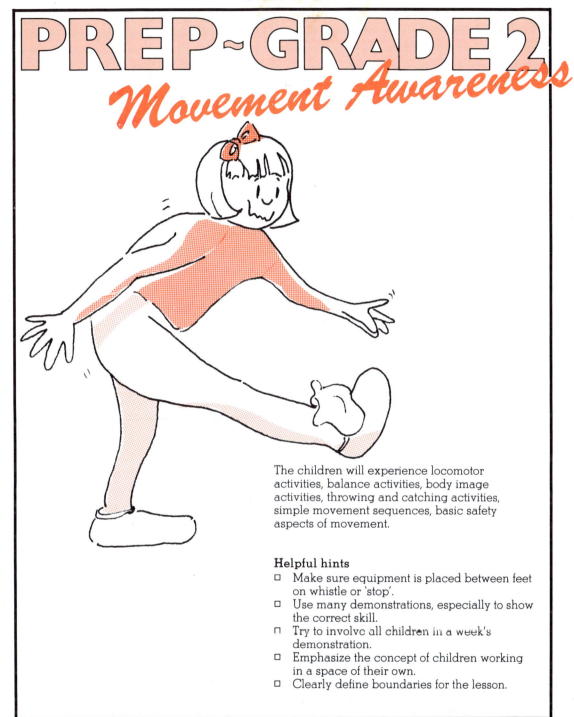

The children will experience locomotor activities, balance activities, body image activities, throwing and catching activities, simple movement sequences, basic safety aspects of movement.

Helpful hints
- ☐ Make sure equipment is placed between feet on whistle or 'stop'.
- ☐ Use many demonstrations, especially to show the correct skill.
- ☐ Try to involve all children in a week's demonstration.
- ☐ Emphasize the concept of children working in a space of their own.
- ☐ Clearly define boundaries for the lesson.

RELATED CLASSROOM ACTIVITIES
- ☐ Same as for ball handling.
- ☐ Combine and/or extend the work and discussion.

LESSON 1

Equipment
A beanbag each.

Warm-up
'Chase your partner', in pairs. On 'go' first child runs into area, on the next 'go' partner chases. Swap over.

Skills
- Holding the beanbag in one hand, hold it very high.
- Hold it very low.
- Hold it between low and high. Discuss a word that could describe this position, e.g. medium.
- Touch your nose with the beanbag. Variations: chin, left ear, hip, ankle, etc.
- Balance the beanbag on your head. Variations: balance on shoulder, hand, elbow, knee, foot, etc.
- Balancing the beanbag on your head, sit down and stand up. Try not to drop the beanbag. Variations: sit down and stand up balancing on different parts of your body.
- Hold the beanbag with: hands, elbows, wrists, knees, ankles. Then see if you can move without dropping the beanbag.

Application
- Relay. Balance the beanbag on your head, walk to line and back. Variations: use different body parts, e.g. hand, foot, finger, etc.

LESSON 2

Equipment
A beanbag each.

Warm-up
In pairs, one child follows the other, moving in a variety of ways, e.g. jumping, skipping, hopping.

Skills
- With the beanbag on the floor, build a bridge over the beanbag using four parts of your body. Variations: using three, then five body parts.
- Make different types of bridges, e.g. long, high, low, wide.
- Gradually bring your bridge lower so your stomach touches the beanbag, then raise it up again.
- Balancing the beanbag on your foot, swing your foot back and forth trying not to drop the beanbag.
- Repeat with the other foot.
- Holding the beanbag in front of you with your hand, kick each leg up to touch the beanbag.
- Sitting on floor with your beanbag between your feet, lift legs up and rock backwards.
- Touch the beanbag on floor behind your head.
- Rock back to sitting position.
- Rock back again and place beanbag on the floor.
- Rock back and pick up beanbag with your feet.

Application
- In groups of eight, circle formation, pass beanbag around circle twice. First team to finish bobs down.

LESSON 3

Equipment
A beanbag each.

Warm-up
Everyone around teacher — run until I blow the whistle, hop back. Variations: jump away, skip back, etc.

Skills
- On the spot, throw up and catch beanbag with both hands.
- Throw up and catch with right hand/left hand.
- Throw up with one hand and catch with the other.
- Try and flip the beanbag like a pancake.
- Passing the beanbag back and forth across the body from hand to hand, follow the movement with your eyes.
- Develop a swing and gradually increase the distance between hands.
- Throw the beanbag in the air, clap your hands once and catch the beanbag.
- Clap hands twice and catch beanbag.
- See how many times you can clap before catching it.
- Throw beanbag ahead of you, then run to catch it.

□ Place beanbag on your foot. Kick beanbag up and try to catch it; change feet.

Application
In groups of four take it in turns to stand in front of group and perform any activity with the beanbag.

Ⓓ □ Other children follow.

LESSON 4

Equipment
A beanbag each.

Warm-up
'Hidden beanbag' — children in free formation with one player in front who throws beanbag over his/her head, counts to ten, turns around and guesses who has the beanbag. If successful he/she has another throw.

Skills
□ Gripping the beanbag with your fingers, raise your arm straight up above your head.
□ Drop the beanbag.
□ Catch it with the other hand.
□ Catch it with the same hand.
□ Repeat with the other hand.
□ Holding the beanbag in your hand, look at a fixed point.
□ Toss and catch the beanbag without moving your eyes.
□ With beanbag placed on head, bend your head forward.
□ Try and catch beanbag with hands when it falls.
□ Repeat; catch with knees, feet.
□ Throw and catch beanbag with eyes closed.
□ Toss the beanbag back and forth from hand to hand while sitting, standing, squatting, lying.
□ Kneel, throw beanbag up and stand up quickly to catch it.

Application
□ Throw the beanbag and try to catch it on top of your head without your hands touching it.

LESSON 5

Equipment
A beanbag and a hoop each.

Warm-up
Children fly around like aeroplanes. On the whistle they land. Last to land stands out each time.

Skills
□ Throwing to a line, throw beanbag over the line.
□ Run and pick it up and bring back to starting position.
□ Repeat with other hand.
□ Throw beanbag into a hoop, using both hands, right hand, left hand.
□ Increase the distance as you get it in the hoop.
□ In groups of three, one person holds the hoop, one throws the beanbag through it and one retrieves beanbag.
□ Rotate places.
□ Take it in turns to throw the beanbags into each successive hoop.
□ Increase the distance between the hoops.

Application
□ In groups of six, each child, one at a time, throws beanbag into each successive hoop.

× × × × × ×   ○ ○ ○ ○ ○ ○

If you miss, you go to the end of the line as normal and the next person has a turn at throwing into your hoop.

LESSON 6

Equipment
A beanbag each.

Warm-up
'Hidden beanbag' — as in Unit 1 Lesson 4.

Skills
□ Place beanbag on the ground, jump over it forwards.
□ Jump over the beanbag backwards.
□ Jump over the beanbag sideways.
□ Hop over the beanbag using both feet and in different directions.
□ Run and jump over the beanbag.
□ Moving at different speeds, move quickly around the beanbag.

- Move very slowly around the beanbag.
- Creep around the beanbag.
- Skip around the beanbag.
- Place one hand on the beanbag, and move around it increasing speed.
- Change hands.
- Place beanbag between your ankles and jump — forwards, backwards, sideways, then in a small circle.

Application
- Place beanbags randomly around area. Children run and jump over as many beanbags as they can in 30 seconds.
- 'Beanbag scramble' — on 'go' collect as many beanbags as you can.

PREP~GRADE 2
Minor Games

The children will experience running/chasing games, imaginative/chanting games, group games/relays, games without equipment, working in a group situation.

Helpful hints
- Set boundaries for your games and make sure everyone understands the instruction.
- Remind children to look where they are running.
- Encourage them to be honest in game situations. Give positive reinforcement.
- Ensure that everyone has a turn at being 'it'. For less skilled children two 'its' can be selected together to keep the game moving.

RELATED CLASSROOM ACTIVITIES
Major theme — animals
- Discuss what type of animals eat each other and why they need to do it. Game, 'Cat chasing mouse', birds eating insects, big fish eating smaller fish.
- Discuss the different types of homes that animals live in, e.g. bears, bees, caterpillars, horses, ducks.
- Discuss animals that can live in the water and also on the land. Game, 'Frogs in the sea'.

Isn't it funny how a bear likes honey buzz buzz buzz I wonder why he does go to sleep bear

LESSON 1

Equipment
Nil.

FIND YOUR PARTNER
Children in two circles, one inside the other.
Partners are opposite each other. The two circles
hop, step, jump, walk, etc. in opposite directions.
On the whistle, all players run to join hands with
their partners and then bob down. The last pair
down is out.

TRAIN CHASEY
Children in pairs with a single player left. Each
pair forms a train, the front the engine and the
back the carriage. The odd player tries to attach
himself/herself to the back of one of the trains. If
successful the engine of that train has to drop off
and attach himself/herself to another train.
Practise this game walking first.

'IS IT DINNERTIME MR WOLF'?
Teacher or a child is Mr Wolf. Mr Wolf is
followed by the class chanting 'is it dinner time
Mr Wolf?'. Mr Wolf gives various answers such
as, 'No it's 9 o'clock, no it's 3 o'clock', but when
he says 'Yes it is' all race home with Mr Wolf
chasing.

CATS AND MICE
Children in a circle holding hands. Two people
stand in the circle being the mice. Another two
stand outside the circle being the cats. The cats
try to catch the mice, but the players hinder the
cats by raising or lowering their arms and not
allowing the cats to break the circle.

BEAR IN THE CAVE
Children stand in a circle holding hands. The
'bear' stands in the middle of the circle. The bear
crawls around and tries to get out of the circle.
The two players holding hands at the spot where
the bear gets out must chase and tag the bear.
The first one to tag is the new bear.

BUSY BEES
Each player has a partner except one being 'it'.
The couples scatter and obey commands such
as 'back to back', 'face each other', 'shake
hands'. On 'busy bees' everyone has to find a
new partner including 'it'. The person without a
partner becomes 'it'.

LESSON 2

Equipment
Nil.

IS IT DINNER TIME MR WOLF?
As in Unit 1 Lesson 1.

CATERPILLAR WALK
Walk forward on hands until body is fully
stretched and legs straight with hips high in the
air. Keep hands still, then walk forward on feet
until they are close to your head.

MONKEY WALK
On feet and hands, all slightly turned in, run
forward, keep knees half bent and the hips
pushed up.

TRAIN CHASEY
As in Unit 1 Lesson 1.

JOCKEYS AND WILD HORSES
Four jockeys are selected and given a stable in
the four corners of the area. Other players gallop
around. On 'go' the jockeys rush out and catch
as many horses as possible, leading each to the
stable (from which they cannot escape) before
catching the next. When all horses are caught,
the jockey with the most horses wins.

CARS AND PEDESTRIANS
Players stand behind a line. On a signal, they
pretend to be cars and drive around the area.
When the teacher calls 'pedestrians' they all run
and stand behind the line, look both ways and
cross the road. Then change back to cars.

CATS AND MICE
As in Unit 1 Lesson 1.

LESSON 3

Equipment
Nil.

SCARECROW CHASEY
Choose about four children to be 'it' at once.
When 'it' tags someone, that child stands in a
wide shape. To be freed, another child must
crawl through the tagged child's legs. Regularly
change those that are 'it'.
Boys versus girls scarecrow chasey.
As above except all girls chase boys and vice
versa.

CAT WALKS

Stretch out right arm and left leg as slowly and as far as possible. Repeat with the other arm and leg.

WILD CATS

As above, but lift hips and keep the legs straight so the weight is on the hands.

BUNNY JUMP

From crouched position move hands forward then spring feet in air to land near hands. The jumps can be quick with small movements or slow with hip lifting.

FROGS IN THE SEA

Two 'frogs' are in the centre of a circle. They jump about while everyone else skips around. They shout 'frogs in the sea can't catch me'. The frogs jump up and chase the rest to a line. When caught the children join the 'frogs' and help catch the others.

JOCKEYS AND WILD HORSES

As in Unit 1 Lesson 2 (p. 18).

GOING FOR A DIP

One side of the line is the sand, the other the sea. Children stand on the sand and pretend to put on their bathers. When ready they run to the line, jump into the sea and swim about. As soon as the whistle goes, they jump out, dry and dress themselves.

LISTEN TO THE WHISTLE

Children move around area. The teacher blows whistle a certain number of times. Children form circles, equal to the number of whistle blows. Anybody left out can help be a judge.

BEAR WALKING

Walk slowly on hands and feet, keeping hands as close as possible to feet. Move hand and leg on the same side together.

DUCK WALKING

Bend knees and waddle forward. A tail can be made with hands, or flap wings by placing the hands under the arm-pits.

LISTEN TO THE WHISTLE

As in Unit 1 Lesson 3.

PLAYING WITH BALLOONS

Everyone has an imaginary balloon. They blow it up until it is very big, hit it around, catch it, etc. On 'pop', they have to burst their balloon and start again.

CARS

In groups of six, relay formation. Players in each team are given names of six cars. When teacher calls out a car name that 'car' from each team runs to the line and back. The first back scores a point for their team. On 'all cars', all players, one at a time starting from the back, crawl through the legs of those in front, then run to line and back. The first team with a straight line wins a point.

Holden	× × × × × ×
Ford	× × × × × ×
Mazda	× × × × × ×
Corona	× × × × × ×
Celica, etc.	× × × × × ×

LESSON 4

Equipment
Nil.

FIND A PARTNER

Choose four children to be 'he' to chase the others. A player is not out if standing with a partner.

LITTLE A BIG A

Children line up at one end of playground while the cat stands with his back turned at other end. They chant:

'Little A' — make yourself as small as possible.
'Big A' — stand as tall as possible.
'Bouncing B' — 3 jumps.
'The cat's in the cupboard and can't catch me' — walk on tiptoe.

The rhyme is repeated until the cat turns and chases. If caught you become a cat and help chase.

LESSON 5

Equipment
Nil.

FIRE, FIRE

One player is the Fire Chief. The other players are divided into three teams, called Fire engines 1, 2, and 3. The Fire Chief calls out 'Fire, fire at... (tree, seat, etc.) fire engine 3 put out the blaze'. Fire engine 3 runs to the spot until 'all clear' is called out by the Chief. The firemen then run back to their station. The first one back being the new Fire Chief. As a surprise, a general alarm can be given and all fire engines are sent out.

GIRAFFE WALKING

Close hands above head to make ears. Walk on tip toes, have a drink of water, then bend down to touch knees with elbows.

THE LION LIMP

Place hands and feet on ground. Hold up right hand and right leg. Jump on left hand and left leg. Swap over.

DUCK WALKING
As in Unit 1 Lesson 4 (p. 19).
LITTLE A BIG A
As in Unit 1 Lesson 4 (p. 19).
CARS
As in Unit 1 Lesson 4 (p. 19).
A WINTER'S DAY
Children follow teacher running like the wind.
Sometimes it is a gentle breeze and sometimes a
gale. When teacher calls 'It's raining' everyone
stops running and pretends to put on raincoats,
hat and gumboots. Then follow the teacher
jumping over the puddles.

LESSON 6

Equipment
Nil.

FIND YOUR PARTNER
As in Unit 1 Lesson 1 (p. 18).
IS IT DINNER TIME MR WOLF?
As in Unit 1 Lesson 1 (p. 18).
BEAR IN THE CAVE
As in Unit 1 Lesson 1 (p. 18). Variation: Have
both children that chase the bear be 'it' next
time, rather than just the one who catches the
bear.
JOCKEYS AND WILD HORSES
As in Unit 1 Lesson 2 (p. 18).
FROGS IN THE SEA
As in Unit 1 Lesson 3 (p. 19).
LISTEN TO THE WHISTLE
As in Unit 1 Lesson 3 (p. 19).
CARS
As in Unit 1 Lesson 4 (p. 19).

PREP~GRADE 2
Gymnastics

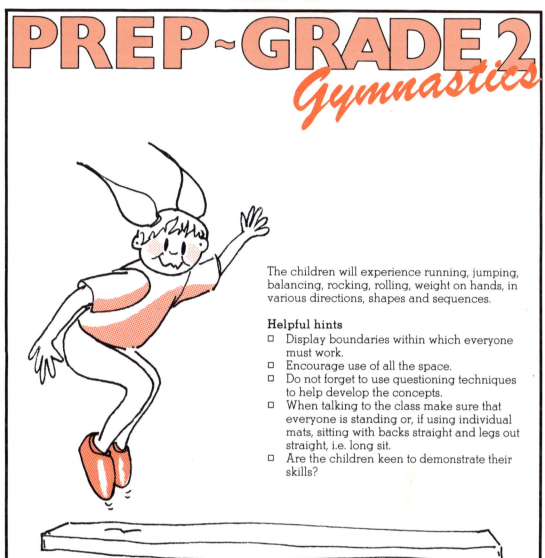

The children will experience running, jumping, balancing, rocking, rolling, weight on hands, in various directions, shapes and sequences.

Helpful hints

- Display boundaries within which everyone must work.
- Encourage use of all the space.
- Do not forget to use questioning techniques to help develop the concepts.
- When talking to the class make sure that everyone is standing or, if using individual mats, sitting with backs straight and legs out straight, i.e. long sit.
- Are the children keen to demonstrate their skills?

RELATED CLASSROOM ACTIVITIES
Major theme — animals

- Make a list of fast moving animals.
- Make a list of slow moving animals.
- What other things can move in different directions? e.g. animals, bikes, cars, toys.
- Draw some ground patterns that you can follow, e.g. forwards, sideways, forwards, sideways, backwards.
- Find a snail and follow its ground pattern.
- Which animals are good jumpers? e.g. kangaroo, horse, dog, monkey, lion.
- Which animals cannot jump? e.g. snakes, snails, turtles.

- Which animals can change their shape? e.g. snails, turtles, cats, worms, dogs.
- Do any animals rock or swing? e.g. monkeys, birds, bats.
- Which animals live under the ground?
- Which animals live underwater?
- Which animals live above the ground?
- Which animals can roll? e.g. horses, bears, dogs, cats, tigers.

LESSON 1

Equipment
A hoop each.

Warm-up
Run forwards. On whistle, run in a different direction.
Run forwards, skip forwards, jump forwards, walk forwards.
Run forwards, hop sideways, jump backwards.
Children run making different ground patterns.
(T) Encourage use of the whole space.

Skills
- From crouch position, jump up and land deeply making sure knees are bent to absorb shock.
- Jump and make a wide shape in air before landing.
- Jump, making various shapes, e.g. thin, twisted, curled.
- Make various shapes, whilst balancing, e.g. thin, curled, twisted, wide.
- Make shapes with various supports, e.g. wide shape with two feet and one hand as body support; curled shape with any two body supports; twisted shape with any four body supports.

(D) Give various demonstrations and encourage variety.

Application
- Wide jump into hoop — forwards, backwards.
- Curled/twisted jump in and out of hoop.
- Introduce a sequence of movements that follow each other.
- Wide jump into hoop, then balance, using three body supports. Twisted jump out.
- Backwards jump in, then wide balance with three body supports. Tall jump out.

LESSON 2

Equipment
A hoop each.

Warm-up
Run forwards, change to running sideways on whistle.
Move in different ways, making different ground patterns.
Follow the person next to you. Try and change directions to lose your partner.

Skills
- Jumping from seat make various shapes, e.g. wide, thin, twisted, turning around.
- Jump to land in hoop, then increase the distance from seat as you get better.
- Jump to land over hoop.
- With a partner, children jump into two consecutive hoops making various shapes, e.g. wide jump, thin jump.
- Balancing, make a curled shape inside your hoop.
- Make a wide shape around your hoop.
- Make a twisted shape, half in and half out of hoop.

Application
- Jump from seats into hoop in a wide shape, then wide jump out.
- Jump into hoop in a twisted shape, then twisted jump out.
- Make up your own sequence.

Give demonstrations and discuss the types of (D) jumps and balances used.

LESSON 3

Equipment
A small gym mat each.

Warm-up
Pretend to be a train, first of all go slowly up a (T) hill, then fast down the hill etc. Allow the children to feel the different speeds from slow, medium, to fast.
Run quickly, hop slowly, then jump medium fast.
Everyone can make up their own pattern.

Skills
- Jump, making wide, thin, curled and twisted shapes and land on the spot.
- Jump with one leg bent and one leg straight.
- Balance on one foot and two hands.
- Balance on two feet and one hand.
- Balance on any three body supports. (D)
- Rock backwards and forwards in any shape.
- Rock in wide shape on bottom and shoulders.
- Rock in wide shape with any body supports.
- Curled roll in any direction.
- Thin roll in sideways direction.
- Forward roll. Squat and sit on heels, hands shoulder-width apart. Lift hips and look through legs. Tuck head and do not put forehead on the mat.

Application
- Any roll followed by a wide shape.
- Thin roll then any shape.

LESSON 4

Equipment
A small gym mat each.

Warm-up
Run quickly forwards, change to jumping backwards slowly.
Run forwards, change to own choice of activity forwards/sideways/backwards.
Jump touching feet in air with one hand/two hands.
Jump in different directions — forwards, backwards, etc.

Skills
- With weight on hands, move two feet and two hands — facing up/facing down.
- Move on two feet and two hands with changes in direction.
- Change from facing up to facing down while moving.
- Revise proper technique for forward roll.
- Roll sideways in a thin shape, then a wide shape.

Application
- Any jump followed by any roll.
- Jump forwards then roll forwards.
- ⒟ Jump sideways then roll sideways.

LESSON 5

Equipment
A small gym mat each.

Warm-up
'Follow the leader' — groups of four to five children follow their leader's actions. Change leaders so everyone has a turn. Encourage different ways of moving, changing direction and speed.

Skills
- ⒟ With a partner, **jump** to meet partner in different shapes. Jump away from partner in different directions.

- Match your partner's **balance** with two, three, four or five body supports.
- Make a partner balance with a total of six, seven or eight body supports.
- One partner in a wide shape, the other in a curled shape. ⒟

Application
- Wide jump to meet a partner, then wide balance.
- Curled jump to meet partner then curled balance.
- Any jump to meet partner, then any balance.

LESSON 6

Equipment
Two long ropes, three hoops, three small mats, six blocks, three canes.

Warm-up
Run to line and then squat like a rabbit.
Jump up, run along line and then squat like a rabbit.
Jump along line and then squat.
Run, then jump up and squat.

Skills/Application
Obstacle circuit
- Children rotate around activities — free play with equipment.
- Children rotate around activities — specified activities as in diagram. Start children at different activities, spend two minutes on each activity and then rotate. Give demonstrations to illustrate variety and how to keep control.
- Jump the snake — jump backwards, jump forwards, jump sideways.

- Walk the tightrope.
- Two foot jumps.

- Rolling — different shapes.

- Jumping over and crawling under.

PREP~GRADE 2
Ball Handling

The children will experience passing, catching, stopping, moving.

Helpful hints

□ Involvement of the teacher is very good motivation for the children.
□ If an activity is too difficult, do not hesitate to modify, and do not persist with it if it is still too hard.
□ When introducing a new game, practise it in slow motion first as this can avoid accidents and misunderstandings.
□ Try and talk to each individual in a lesson.
□ Keep up the demonstrations, especially where the children are creating their own movements.

RELATED CLASSROOM ACTIVITIES
Major theme — games

□ Discuss and make a list of games that use different body parts, e.g. legs — football; hands — netball, cricket, etc.
□ Discuss different things that move along the ground, e.g. cars, bikes, various animals, balls.
□ Discuss different things that move through the air, e.g. birds, aeroplanes, balls, etc.

□ Which things go along the ground and through the air? e.g. balls, birds, areoplanes, etc.
□ In which games are the skills mainly in the air? e.g. football, netball, Newcombe.
□ In which games are the skills mainly on the ground? e.g. bowls, ten pin bowling, hockey, etc.

LESSON 1

Equipment
One large ball between two.

Warm-up
Run around the area, change direction on the whistle, taking care to avoid bumping into others.

Skills
(D)
- Pass the ball in different ways to a partner.
- Count how many different ways you can pass the ball.
- Pass the ball using different body parts. Discuss the body parts being used.
- Count how many body parts you use.
- Practise your favourite way of passing the ball. Try and make it go straight to your partner.
- Pass the ball so it stays on the ground, e.g. roll, push, kick.
- Pass the ball on the ground using different body parts.
- Pass the ball on the ground, then in the air, straight to your partner.

Application
- Ball and jump race, in relay formation. Children stand behind a line. A ball is placed opposite each line at the other end. On signal, one player at a time runs to the ball, places it between their feet and jumps back to the starting line.

LESSON 2

Equipment
One large ball between two.

Warm-up
With a partner, follow Unit 1, Lesson 1 — Minor games (p. 18).

Skills
(T)
- Pass the ball in different ways to a partner. Teacher should encourage different body parts on the ground, etc.
- Pass the ball along the ground.

(D)
- Practise ways of passing the ball in the air.
- Stand close to your partner and pass the ball. Each time you pass it without touching the ground, take a step back. If the ball touches the ground take a step forward.

Application
- In circles of five or six, with one ball for each circle. Pass the ball around three times racing against each other in the following ways: while standing, while sitting, using your feet, etc.

LESSON 3

Equipment
One ball between two.

Warm-up
Train chasey — as in Unit 1, Lesson 1 — Minor games (p. 18).

Skills
- Pass the ball along the ground to a partner using different body parts.
- Find different ways of stopping the ball. (D)
- Count the number of ways you can stop the ball.
- Pass the ball so your partner has to move to stop it.
- Move along as you pass the ball to your partner.
- Practise your favourite way of passing and stopping as you move.
- Try to move as fast as you can while still passing and stopping.

Application
- 'Dodge ball' — One team forms a circle and the others stand in this circle in free formation. Team forming the circle tries to hit any of the dodging players below the knee. When a player is hit, he or she joins in the circle. The game may continue until all players have been hit, or have a time limit for each team, the winning team having the most number of players left in at the end of the time.

LESSON 4

Equipment
One ball between two.

Warm-up
'Is it dinner time Mr Wolf?' — as in Unit 1, Lesson 1 — Minor games (p. 18).

Skills
- ☐ With a partner, practise passing and stopping the ball in different ways.
- ☐ Pass the ball, keeping it in the air, using different body parts.
- ☐ Keep walking while you pass the ball.
- Ⓓ ☐ Practise your best pass while you are moving — no stopping to pass the ball.
- ☐ Throw the ball into the air so your partner has to run to stop it. Swap over.

Application
- ☐ 'Fielding relay' — Relay formation, one ball per team. Each player in turn rolls the ball across the line which is 10 metres away, retrieves it and passes back to the next player in line.
- ☐ 'Who's hiding the ball?' — Children stand in free formation behind a player holding a ball. This player throws the ball overhead, counts to ten and tries to guess who has it. If successful he or she has another turn; if not, the player with the ball takes his or her place.

LESSON 5

Equipment
One ball between two.

Warm-up
Find your partner — as in Unit 1, Lesson 1 (p. 18).

Skills
- Ⓓ ☐ Pass the ball to a partner keeping it in the air and using different body parts.
- ☐ Pass the ball only using your hands.

- ☐ Using your hands, pass the ball straight to your partner.
- ☐ Find different ways of passing the ball straight to your partner.
- ☐ Pass the ball away from your partner so he/she has to run to stop it.

Application
- ☐ 'Dodge ball' — as in Unit 2, Lesson 3 (p. 25).

LESSON 6

Equipment
One ball between two.

Warm-up
'Scarecrow chasey' — as in Unit 1, Lesson 3 — Minor games (p. 18).

Skills
- ☐ Practise the different ways you can stop the ball.
- ☐ Practise different ways of catching the ball, e.g. one or two hands, high, low.
- ☐ Pass the ball so your partner has to move to catch it.

Give teaching points for catching the ball, 'watch the ball', 'move to the ball'. Ⓣ
- ☐ Bounce the ball and catch it with your hands.
- ☐ Pass the ball in the air to partner and catch it in different ways.

Application
- ☐ 'Scramble'. Groups of five, one ball to each group. One person in each group throws the ball and the rest of the group attempts to catch it. The successful person scores 1 point.
- ☐ 'Who's hiding the ball?' — as in Unit 2, Lesson 4.

Using Hoops

PREP~GRADE 2
Movement Awareness

The children will experience drama activities, speed and agility activities, walking, leaping, hopping, skipping — with a rope.

Helpful hints
- Questioning techniques can be used to make sure the children understand the task.
- Give positive reinforcement to correct behaviour.
- Be aware of less skilled children and make them feel a sense of achievement by setting individual goals.
- Make sure equipment is between feet on ground on 'stop' or the whistle.
- Teacher interest and involvement has a very positive effect on the lesson.

RELATED CLASSROOM ACTIVITIES
Major theme — the farm
- Farm animals — various activities could be incorporated. What animals are on a farm? Why do farmers need these animals?
- Living on a farm — what jobs do Dad, Mum, children have? What different types of farms are there?
- Going to school in the country — how would you get to school? How big would the school be? How many teachers would there be?

LESSON 1

Equipment
A beanbag each.

Warm-up
Story game — 'We live on a farm'. The teacher tells the story and the children standing in a circle imitate the story.

Story	Action
We get out of bed at 6 o'clock	Stretch and yawn.
Jump up and down to warm up	Jump in place.
Breathe fresh air from window.	Breathe deeply.
Run outside to the hayshed.	Run on spot.
Climb into the hay.	Pretend to climb.
Leap about in the hay.	High jumps.
Go to the cattle.	Run and skip.
Chase the cattle home.	Run.

Skills
Speed is an important factor in the following.
- Pass the beanbag quickly around your waist in one direction, with eyes closed, change direction.
- Pass the beanbag from one hand to the other in front and behind the body, with eyes closed.
- Pass the beanbag around your head, change direction, with eyes closed.
- Pass the beanbag in and out and around your knees. Then try variations as above.
- Balance on right foot and pass beanbag around your left knee. Repeat with the other leg.
- With beanbag on head, bend backwards until it falls down. Reach between your legs and pick up the beanbag. Repeat, doing it as fast as you can.

Application
- 'Three blind mice' — children move around in circle chanting the rhyme. At any time a player in the middle claps hands (farmer's wife) and chases the rest home. A new farmer's wife is chosen.

LESSON 2

Equipment
A rhythm stick (or similar) each.

Warm-up
Story game 'We live on a farm' — as in Unit 2, Lesson 1.

Skills
- Holding the stick in your hand, move it in both directions using your fingers, then swap hands.
- Hold the stick horizontally and use your fingers to move it, then reverse direction. See how quickly you can move your fingers.
- Holding the stick vertically, crawl your fingers up and down the stick.
- Repeat with other hand.
- Sit on the ground and spin the stick on the ground.
- Change directions and hands.
- Sitting with your knees bent, let your fingers make the stick roll around your body and under your knees. Change it from hand to hand.

Application
- Relays — run up to line with stick and back again. Walk up to line and back passing the stick around your body. Run up to line and back passing the stick from hand to hand.

LESSON 3

Equipment
A rhythm stick (or similar) each.

Warm-up
Walking, make different patterns on the ground, e.g. circles, triangles.
Walk tall then small.
Walk as heavily as an elephant.
Walk as lightly as a bird.
Walk with a happy then a sad face.
Walk like a cat, duck.

Skills
- Toss the stick from hand to hand.
- Lift the stick above your head. Let it go and try to catch it with the same hand. Repeat with the other hand.

- Flip the stick in the air and catch it with the opposite/same hand. Repeat with the other hand.
- Hold the stick horizontally with hands at each end. Raise the stick to eye level with arms straight. Let the stick go and try to catch it. Repeat, using separate hands.
- With one stick between two, pass it to each other as many times as you can in 30 seconds then 1 minute.
- Stand back to back and pass stick to partner, collect it from the other side, then pass stick around and around as many times as you can in 30 seconds then 1 minute.
- Stand back to back and pass stick between legs then above head as many times as you can in 30 seconds then 1 minute.

Application
- Story game, 'We live on a farm' — as in Unit 2, Lesson 1 (p. 28).

Through the mud	'Doing, doing'
Around the trees	'Swish, swish'
Through the grass	BANG!
Back home and slam the door	

Skills
- Run around and on signal, **leap** over a puddle.
- Run around and on signal, leap as high as you can.
- Run and on signal, leap to bring your knees to your chest.
- As above, but clap under your knees.
- Using a skipping rope, children one at a time jump over a still/moving rope.
- One at a time, run through a turning rope.

Application
Story game, 'We live on a farm' — as in Unit 2, Lesson 1 (p. 28).

LESSON 4

Equipment
Long skipping rope.

Warm-up
Ⓓ Story game, 'The lion hunt'. Children repeat words and relevant actions after the teacher.

Story	Action
Going on a lion hunt	Walk in circle
Going to catch a big one	
I'm not scared	Hands to eyes — look
Don't see any lions yet	
Oh! Oh!	Brush hands back and forth
Deep grass	
Have to go through it	Make a swish noise
Oh! Oh!	
Trees	
Big tall trees	'Doing, doing'
Have to go around them	'Doing, doing'
Oh! Oh!	Lift feet and shlurp
Through the mud	Shlurp, shlurp, shlurp
Oh! Oh!	Stoop and walk in
I see a cave	'Oo, oo, oo, oo'
A dark gloomy cave	
Have to go through it	
I see one eye	
I see two eyes	
It's a lion	'Oo, oo'
Back through the cave	'Shlurp, shlurp

LESSON 5

Equipment
Long skipping rope.

Warm-up
Story game, 'The lion hunt' — as in Unit 2, Lesson 4.

Skills
- Leaping (revise activities in Unit 2, Lesson 4).
- Hopping — hop in area, on signal change feet.
- Hop to a pattern, e.g. 4 left foot, 4 right foot; 10 left foot, 10 right foot.
- Hop out a letter of the alphabet.
- Try hopping with one hand on your knee and the other on your head.
- Skipping — using long skipping rope, revise Unit 2, Lesson 4.
- Try to make the running through continuous, e.g. miss two loops, run through, miss two loops, run through, etc.

Application
- 'The mermaid of the sea' — children chant 'Mermaid of the sea, you can't catch me'. Mermaid replies 'Yes I can if you walk' (hop, skip, run, leap, etc.). Players then try to get across the sea, being chased by the mermaid who performs the same action as the players. Choose someone else to be the mermaid.

LESSON 6

Equipment
Four short ropes, one large ruler.

Warm-up
Story game, 'The lion hunt' — as in Unit 2,
Lesson 4 (p. 29).

Skills/Application
- 'Skipping the sea' — form a double circle,
  and four pairs spread around the circle have
  a rope which they hold between them (see
  diagram). The rest of the players move
  around the circle, trying not to let the rope
  touch them. The teacher stands in the middle
  and calls directions:
     'Skip the choppy sea' (rope up and down)
     'Skip the flowing sea' (rope back and forth)
     'Skip the low sea' (rope is low)
     'Skip the high sea' (under a high rope)
  The pair about to jump the high sea, take over
  the rope and the game begins again.

- Magic stick — the teacher holds the stick
  (ruler) and tells the children what to do, i.e.
  hop, skip, etc. When the stick is hidden
  behind the teacher's back the children run
  for home. Those caught help chase next time.
- Circus acts — children move around circle
  doing actions as stated by the teacher, e.g.
  run, hop, etc. On 'stop' the children do the
  action of a stated circus animal, e.g. horse,
  lion, etc. On 'go' children continue hopping
  or whatever the action was.

PREP~GRADE 2

Minor Games

The children will experience running and chasing games, imaginative and chanting games, group games and relays, games with limited equipment, working in a group situation.

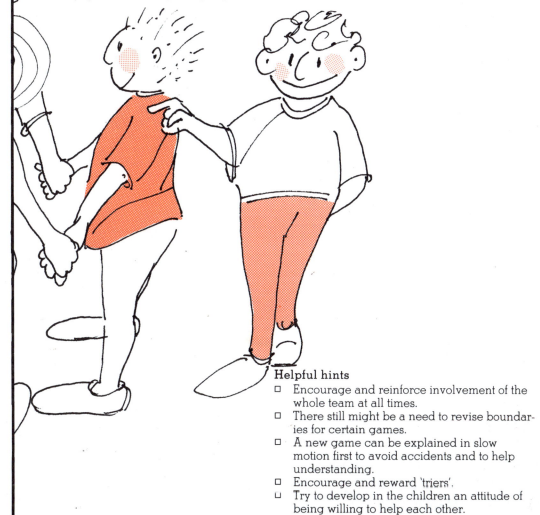

Helpful hints

- ☐ Encourage and reinforce involvement of the whole team at all times.
- ☐ There still might be a need to revise boundaries for certain games.
- ☐ A new game can be explained in slow motion first to avoid accidents and to help understanding.
- ☐ Encourage and reward 'triers'.
- ☐ Try to develop in the children an attitude of being willing to help each other.
- ☐ Make sure everyone is listening and watching when a game is being explained.

RELATED CLASSROOM ACTIVITIES

Major theme — farm/animals

- ☐ In the game 'Crumbs or crusts' what other words could be used? e.g. rabbits or rascals.
- ☐ Which animals are useful on a farm? e.g. sheep dog, sheep, chicken, etc.
- ☐ Which animals are 'enemies' of the farmer? e.g. rabbits, wolves, etc.
- ☐ List all the animals that can walk, e.g. from the games — pigeons, cats, mice, ducks, monkeys, rabbits.

LESSON 1

Equipment
Nil.

CRUMBS OR CRUSTS
Children are in two lines, one metre apart, facing each other. One line is called 'crumbs' and the other 'crusts'. The teacher calls out a name; if 'crumbs' is called, that line runs away and 'crusts' chase. Any children caught before crossing a given line change sides.

WALK OR RUN
Children in circle facing centre. Two children are 'its' and walk around the outside of the circle chanting 'walk, walk, walk…' tapping each child on the shoulder as they pass them. When they say 'run' the players touched chase them around the circle and back to the chaser's spot. The chasers become the new 'its'.

IS IT DINNER TIME MR WOLF?
As in Unit 1, Lesson 1 — Minor games (p. 18).

BILLY BOYD
Children are in two lines facing each other, each child opposite a partner. Both lines repeat the following rhyme with actions:

Story	Action
'Billy Boyd' can jump.	All jump
'Billy Boyd' can hop.	All hop
But when my Billy starts to run	The two leaders run down the centre, round the lines and back to their place. First child back gets a point for the team.
Why he never stops.	

The verse is repeated for each couple.

LESSON 2

Equipment
A beanbag each.

IS IT DINNER TIME MR WOLF?
As in Unit 1, Lesson 1 — Minor games (p. 18).

ACROSS THE RIVER
Relay formation. Leaders with a beanbag. A space of 2 metres is marked some distance in front of the teams. The leaders throw the beanbag across the river, run to pick it up and throw it back to the next player. The first team to finish wins.

UNDER THE GATES
Relay teams make the shape shown in the diagram with gates at the top. On 'go' each team runs under its gate, around a specified area outside the gate leg, up to a line and back through its gate to line up. Variation: each child has a beanbag and once outside the gate, throws up the beanbag and catches it ten times before going back through the gates.

WALK OR RUN
As in Unit 2, Lesson 1.

CATS AND MICE
As in Unit 1, Lesson 1 — Minor Games (p. 18).

THE WOLF AND THE SHEEP
Children organized as shown in diagram. When the wolf claps his hands, the sheep try to run from one line to the other without being caught. If caught they become wolves. Only the original wolf can give the clap to bring the sheep out.

LESSON 3

Equipment
Nil

THE WOLF AND THE SHEEP
As in Unit 2, Lesson 2.
CRUMBS OR CRUSTS
As in Unit 2, Lesson 1 (p. 32).
BIRDS IN THE TREES
Divide class into groups of three. Two children join hands to represent hollow trees and the third stands between them to represent birds. Have a couple of extra birds without a home. At a given signal all birds change trees. The odd birds attempt to get a tree during the change. Change trees so everyone can be a bird.
THE HUNTER
One child is the hunter and says to the others, 'Come with me to hunt lions'. Everyone follows. When the hunter says 'Bang' the other children run to the line as the hunter tries to tag as many as possible. As each person is tagged the hunter calls out his or her name. The hunter chooses a replacement from the players who reached home safely.
GIANTS CHASE FAIRIES
Children are divided into two groups standing at each end of the area. One represents 'Giants' and the other 'Fairies'. The teacher calls 'Fairies' who come out and dance around. When 'Giants' is called, the fairies run for home and the giants chase. If caught the fairies become giants. Roles can also be changed.

LESSON 4

Equipment
Nil

THE HUNTER
As in Unit 2, Lesson 3.
WALK OR RUN
As in Unit 2, Lesson 1 (p. 32).
CRUMBS OR CRUSTS
As in Unit 2, Lesson 1 (p. 32).
CATS AND MICE
As in Unit 1, Lesson 1 — Minor games (p. 18).
TOP AND BOTTOM
Children to be in four lines. When teacher calls 'top', the leaders stand still while all the team

race around him/her and return to their places. On 'bottom' the last person in the team stands still and all the team race around him/her and back to their places. Variations: hop, skip, jump; without touching anyone.

LESSON 5

Equipment
Nil.

FARMER JOE AND THE RABBITS
The children bunny-hop around the area. Farmer Joe comes with three or four dogs (children running on hands and feet). The dogs chase the rabbits and try to tag as many as they can before the farmer calls them away.
BILLY BOYD
As in Unit 2, Lesson 1 (p. 32).
TOP AND BOTTOM
As in Unit 2, Lesson 4.
CRUMBS OR CRUSTS
As in Unit 2, Lesson 1 (p. 32).
RUN RABBIT RUN HOME
Children in two groups called foxes and rabbits. The rabbits are safe in their homes. The foxes walk about the forest (area). Mother rabbit takes her children out. They tiptoe quietly for the fox might be near. Suddenly the leader of the foxes calls out 'run rabbit run home'. All the rabbits run for home while the foxes try to tag them. Those caught become foxes.

LESSON 6

Equipment
Nil.

FARMER JOE AND THE RABBITS
As in Unit 2, Lesson 5.
RUN RABBIT RUN HOME
As in Unit 2, Lesson 5.
TOP AND BOTTOM
As in Unit 2, Lesson 4.
BIRDS IN THE TREES
As in Unit 2, Lesson 3.
WALK OR RUN
As in Unit 2, Lesson 1 (p. 32).
CRUMBS OR CRUSTS
As in Unit 2, Lesson 1 (p. 32).

PREP~GRADE 2
Gymnastics

The children will experience running, jumping, balancing, rolling, weight on hands — with emphasis on equipment and sequences.

Helpful hints
- Allow the children to develop their natural tendency to explore.
- This is an excellent unit in which to encourage the children to help coach each other.
- With group work, regularly stop the whole class and give demonstrations.
- Another discipline control is to pre-warn a group they will be demonstrating in two minutes. This keeps them on their toes.
- Are the children enjoying P. E.?

RELATED CLASSROOM ACTIVITIES
Major theme — animals
- Which animals can kick or lift their legs? e.g. horse, donkey, dog, monkey.
- Which animals can use their back as a body support? e.g. horse, dog, elephant, lion.
- Which animals could crawl through your legs when playing scarecrow chasey?
- Which animals could not crawl through your legs when playing scarecrow chasey?
- The circus animals — which animals could be trained to walk across the balance beam? Which animals spring like you do off the spring board? Which animals could jump over the vaulting horse? Are there any that could crawl over the vaulting horse? The circus acts could be compared to the gymnastic acts of the children.

LESSON 1

Equipment
Small gym mat each.

Warm-up
Running — with long steps, with short steps, with a partner keeping in time, with each other.

Skills
- Jumping in different directions, forwards, backwards, sideways.
- Jumping to touch feet while in the air.
- Any type of balance with your head facing up.
- Any type of balance with your head facing down.
- Any type of balance with your head sideways.
- Balance on three body supports with arm as the highest point.
- Balance on four body supports with knee as the highest point.
- Revise the forward roll technique.
- Roll in various directions, forwards, backwards, etc.

Application
- Sequence development — any curled roll followed by your own choice of jump.
- Any curled roll then own choice of balance.
- As above except with a partner.
- Partner sequence — a roll then a jump followed by a balance.

LESSON 2

Equipment
Ten canes, twenty blocks, trampet, three or four large mats.

Warm-up
With a partner, run and jump at different speeds trying to keep as close as possible together. 'Catch your horse' — one person runs out into area being the horse. On a signal, the partner (jockey) runs out to catch the horse.

Skills
- Canes and blocks are spread around area, children have free jumps over the canes.
- Let them see how many different ways they can get over the canes, e.g. standing jump, running jump, scissor jump, cartwheels, backwards jump.

Application
In two groups:
1. Jump off trampet with teacher supervision.
2. Free exploration — stepping onto trampet, walk and jump, run and jump.

Take off with one foot on the ground and two feet ⓣ on trampet. Jump up and not forward.
1. Jump making various shapes in the air, wide, thin, curled.
2. Let children practise any type of **roll**. Sequence — roll then jump; roll then balance. Swap over groups halfway through time.

× × × × × ×   ☐

× × × × × ×   ☐

× × × × × ×   ☐

LESSON 3

Equipment
Balance beam, trampet, two beanbags.

Warm-up
'Scarecrow chasey' — as in Unit 1, Lesson 1 — Minor games (p. 18). Emphasize wide shapes. ⓣ

Skills
With weight on hands, keeping hands on the spot, move around on feet.
- Keeping feet on the spot, move around on hands.
- Free practice of weight on hands only, lifting feet into air.

Hands should be flat, head should be kept back. ⓣ
- Balancing — children step up onto balance beam and walk across it.

Introduce various safety aspects such as: concentration, watching the beam, not the spectators.

Application
In two groups:
1. Jump off trampet — as in Unit 3, Lesson 2.
2. Walk across balance beam — forwards, sideways.

□ Crawl across, balance beam.
□ Travel along beam balancing a beanbag on head.
Swap groups halfway through.

LESSON 4

Equipment
Springboard, one large mat, balance beam, one ball, one cane.

Warm-up
'Catch your horse' — as in Unit 3, Lesson 2 (p. 35).

Skills
□ With weight on hands, revise kicking up legs — as in Unit 3, Lesson 3 (p. 35).
□ Children run and jump up in the air, taking off on one foot and landing on two. Bend knees on landing.

Application
Divide class into two groups.
1 With teacher supervision, walk up to springboard then step on and jump off.
Ⓣ Take off on one foot, land on two feet with knees bent.
□ Run up to springboard and jump.
□ Run up and jump, various shapes, over the cane.
2 Revise balance beam exercises as in Unit 3, Lesson 3 (p. 35).
□ Walk backwards along beam.
□ Walk with heel to toe, heel to toe.
□ Walk with the left foot always in front of the right.
□ Walk, pick up the ball and carry it to the end.
Swap groups halfway through.

LESSON 5

Equipment
Small mat each, springboard, ten hoops, vaulting horse.

Warm-up
'Giants chase fairies' — as in Unit 2, Lesson 3 — Minor games (p. 33).

Skills
□ Weight on hands, introduce frogstand.

Kneel on knees; sit back on heels; place hands Ⓣ so fingers are in line with knees; lean forward and place head on mat; raise hips and place knees, one at a time on elbows.

Application
In two groups:
1 Practise frogstand with a partner.
□ Practise rolling through a hoop held by partner.
2 Springboard and vaulting horse (low level), with teacher supervision, walk to springboard, climb onto vaulting horse (low level) and jump off.
□ Walk to springboard, jump with hands on horse and lift hips high.
□ Those children who are ready can try 'side squat'.
Stand sideways to horse; place hands on the Ⓣ horse; bounce hips up and lift knees and place feet on bench.
□ Children who are very confident can go all the way over — i.e. 'front vault'.

LESSON 6

Equipment
Springboard, vaulting horse, ten small mats.

Warm-up
'Frogs in the sea' — as in Unit 1, Lesson 3 (p. 19).

Skills/Application
Rotate children around three areas revising all activities.
1 Jumping, using springboard and horse (with teacher supervision) as in Unit 3, Lesson 5.
2 Balancing, using beam, as in Unit 3, Lesson 4.
3 Weight on hands/rolling. With a partner, frogstand, as in Unit 3, Lesson 5.
□ Rolling in various directions.
□ Balances — frogstand — as in Unit 3, Lesson 5.

UNIT 3

PREP~GRADE 2
Ball Handling

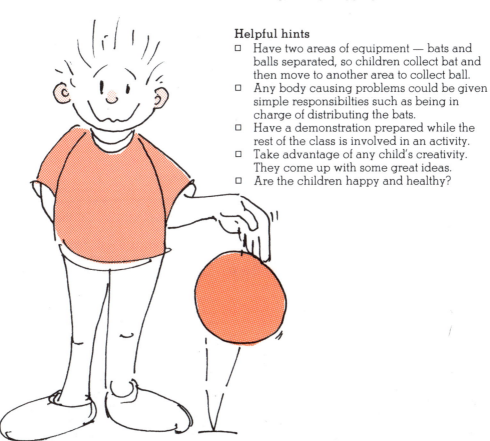

The children will experience hitting, bouncing, dribbling, rolling, stopping — all with a bat.

Helpful hints
- Have two areas of equipment — bats and balls separated, so children collect bat and then move to another area to collect ball.
- Any body causing problems could be given simple responsibilties such as being in charge of distributing the bats.
- Have a demonstration prepared while the rest of the class is involved in an activity.
- Take advantage of any child's creativity. They come up with some great ideas.
- Are the children happy and healthy?

RELATED CLASSROOM ACTIVITIES
Major theme — games
- How many different bats are there? e.g. cricket, rounders, bat-tennis, softball, baseball, table-tennis
- What other equipment do we hit with? e.g. hockey stick, tennis racquet, squash racquet, ice-hockey stick, polo stick, croquet stick.
- Sketch all the shapes of bats, sticks and racquets. e.g.

- Many classroom activities could be related to these basic shapes.

LESSON 1

Equipment
big holey ball 7

Five hoops, one small ball (15 cm) each.

Warm-up
'Is it dinner time Mr Wolf'? As in Unit 1, Lesson 1 — Minor games (p. 18).

Skills
- ☐ Move the ball around using your feet.
- ☐ Move the ball around using your hands.
- ☐ Use one hand then change to the other.
- Ⓓ ☐ Hit the ball with your hand by dropping the ball with one hand and hitting it with the other.
- ☐ Hit the ball in as many directions as you can.
- ☐ Try to bounce the ball.
- Ⓣ Try not to have a stiff hand, it is more like a push than a hard hit. See how many bounces you can get in a row.
  - ☐ With a partner, standing about two to three metres apart, bounce the ball to each other so it bounces in the middle. Gradually increase distance as skill increases.

Application
'Ball scramble' — four teams as in diagram. Each player one at a time runs to collect a ball and bounces it back to their hoop. Balls can be taken from the centre hoop or from another team's hoop.

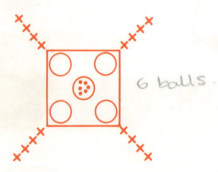

6 balls

LESSON 2

Equipment
One bat each, one small ball each.

Warm-up
'Scarecrow chasey' — as in Unit 1, Lesson 3 — Minor games (p. 18).

Skills
- ☐ Allow free exploration with bat and ball.
- ☐ Move the ball with the bat in different ways, e.g. bouncing, hitting, pushing. Ⓓ
- ☐ Use different parts of the bat to move the ball.
- ☐ Move the ball close to the ground.
- ☐ Keep the ball off the ground. Ⓓ

Application
- ☐ 'Ball scramble' — as in Unit 3, Lesson 1.
- ☐ Relays — hitting the ball along the ground to line and back; bouncing the ball with bat to line and back.

LESSON 3

Equipment
One bat and ball each.

Warm-up
'Crumbs or crusts' — as in Unit 2, Lesson 1 — Minor games (p. 32).

Skills
- ☐ Move the ball with the bat, then change hands.
- ☐ Try hitting the ball with different parts of the bat — along the ground, in the air.
- ☐ With the bat keep the ball close to the ground, e.g. low bouncing, rolling.
- ☐ Develop a sequence with the bat — ball in the air, ball in the air, ball on the ground, ball on the air, ball on the ground, etc. Ⓓ
- ☐ As above but while moving around the area.

Application
- ☐ 'Passing versus hitting' — two teams as in diagram. On 'go' number 1 from the line runs around circle hitting ball with bat, while the circle team try to pass the ball as many times as they can. When number 1 from the line completes his circuit, number 2 goes and so on until all members have had a turn. When finished teams swap over and see who scores the highest number of passes.

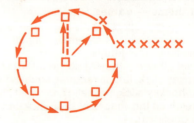

LESSON 4

Equipment
One bat and ball each, five hoops.

Warm-up
'Is it dinner time Mr Wolf? — as in Unit 1, Lesson 1 — Minor games (p. 18).

Skills
- Move the ball with the bat close to the ground and in different directions.
- Hit the ball along the ground away from you, then run after it and stop it with your bat.
- Repeat above but run in front of the ball to stop it.
- Roll ball to partner who stops it with the bat.
- Count the number of different ways you can stop the ball with your bat.
- Make your partner move to stop the ball.
- (T) Move behind the line of the ball to stop it. Watch the ball all the time.
- Pass the ball to partner who hits it back.
- Find different ways of hitting it back.

Application
- 'Ball scramble' — as in Unit 3, Lesson 1 (p. 38).
- Variation — everyone has their own bat, and pat bounces the ball back to their hoop.

LESSON 5

Equipment
A bat and ball each.

Warm-up
'Scarecrow chasey' — as in Unit 1, Lesson 3 — Minor games (p. 18).

Skills
- Free exploration with bat and ball. On signal change bat to other hand.
- Drop ball on ground and hit it with bat in different directions.
- Introduce bouncing. Keep hitting the ball onto the ground.
- (T) Push the ball down with you bat, try not to hit hard.
- Walk around the area while bouncing the ball.
- Hit the ball hard, softly, slowly (ball has to go high), quickly (ball stays low).

Application
- Four teams in relay formation. Walk to line, bouncing the ball with the bat. Run to line, bouncing the ball with the bat. Front person bounces ball around team and back to place, passes ball and bat to number 2 who continues.
- Variation — weave in and out of team.

LESSON 6

Equipment
A bat and ball each; a hoop each.

Warm-up
'Crumbs or crusts' — as in Unit 2, Lesson 1 — Minor games (p. 32).

Skills
- Move around bouncing the ball with the bat.
- Bounce the ball quickly then slowly, high then low.
- Each person has a hoop, and hits the ball in and out of the hoop, e.g. 5 hits in, 5 hits out and so on.
- Bounce the ball around the hoop.
- Bounce the ball quickly inside the hoop, and slowly outside the hoop.

Application
- 'Musical hoops' — leave hoops scattered around area. Children move around hoops bouncing ball with the bat. On whistle children jump in a hoop with the last one missing out. Remove one or two hoops each time until only a few are left.
- 'Bounce the river' — each person has a bat and ball and sits with legs straight. When their number is called they bounce their ball over the legs to the top of the line, down the side and back to their place. First back gets a point for their team.

UNIT 3

PREP ~ GRADE 2
Movement Awareness

The children will experience drama and agility activities, skipping with a long rope, hopscotch, locomotor movements — skipping, sliding, galloping, jumping.

Helpful hints

- Select different children to hold the end of the rope for skipping.
- Change children regularly as their arms tire very quickly.
- Try to develop cooperation among the children when in smaller groups.
- Is everyone keen to demonstrate what they can do?

RELATED CLASSROOM ACTIVITIES

Major theme — 'old time' games

- What sort of games did children play in the colonial days? e.g. hopscotch, kick the can, skipping, apple biting, playing with hoops.
- Hopscotch — how were their courts made? Did they have asphalt?

- What do we do in our spare time? The place of television as compared with playing outside. This could lead to various graph work.

LESSON 1

Equipment
Rhythm stick (or similar) each.

Warm-up
Story game — 'One day at camp'. The teacher tells the story and the children act it out.

Story	Actions
Get-up bell rings.	Stretch and yawn
Jump out of bed.	Big jump.
Morning dip.	Run to lake, jump in, swim about.
Back to camp to chop wood for fire.	Using the axe.
Eat breakfast.	
Go canoeing.	Paddle canoe.
Rest time.	Lie down and go to sleep.

Skills
- □ Balancing the stick — with four fingers, then three, then two fingers.
- □ Repeat with other hand.
- □ Balance stick on your head, chin, forehead, shoulder, knee, foot.
- □ Balance stick vertically on your palm, fingers.
- □ Repeat with other hand.
- □ Balance stick on shoulder and walk in various directions.
- □ As above, except on various body parts.

Application
- □ Nursery rhyme 'Little Bo Peep'.

Words	Actions
1 Little Bo Peep has lost her sheep	Clap legs 4 times, clap hands 4 times.
2 And doesn't know where to find them	Shake head.
3 Leave them alone and they will come home	Walk in circle.
4 Wagging their tails behind them.	Wag tail.

Repeat as above, except line 3. Variation: skip in circle; skip with partner.

LESSON 2

Equipment
A rhythm stick each, long skipping rope.

Warm-up
Story game 'One day at camp' — as in Unit 3, Lesson 1.

Skills
- □ Holding the stick, pass it around your body, change directions.
- □ Pass it under your knees to the other hand.
- □ Trace a pattern of eight with the stick around your knees. ⓓ

See how many circuits children can do in one minute. ⓣ
- □ Holding stick horizontally with two hands, see if you can step forwards over it. See if you can now go back again.
- □ One at a time, jump over 'wriggly' rope.
- □ Run through turning rope.
- □ Try and make it continuous, e.g. miss one or two loops depending on the children's ability.

Application
'Little Bo Peep' — as in Unit 3, Lesson 1.

LESSON 3

Equipment
Long skipping rope.

Warm-up
'The mermaid of the sea' — as in Unit 2, Lesson 5 — Movement awareness (p. 29).

Skills
- □ Skip forwards, backwards, sideways.
- □ Change directions on a signal.
- □ Start vey slowly and gradually get faster.
- □ Skip with high knees, so you can slap them. ⓣ

Skip on your toes.
Swing the opposite arm to leg.
Try and skip lightly and high.
- □ Skipping, with long rope, revise as in Unit 3, Lesson 2.
- □ Introduce running into rope, jumping, running out.

Application
- □ 'Stop' — teacher points in one direction and calls 'skip'. On 'stop' all children must stop

41

immediately. Anyone moving drops out.
- Variation — other movements can be used, e.g. hopping, jumping, etc.

LESSON 4

Equipment
A long ruler.

Warm-up
'Three blind mice' — as in Unit 2, Lesson 1 — Movement awareness (p. 28).

Skills
(D) Demonstrate sliding from one foot to the other.
- Try and slide smoothly.
- Make up a pattern to slide in — a circle, square, etc.
- Start with small slides and gradually make them bigger.
- Slide at different speeds.
- Slide with a partner — following, side by side, back to back.
- Make up a sequence, slide, then skip, then walk.
(D) □ Partners make up their own sequences.
- Can you touch your head while you slide?
- Repeat touching different body parts.

Application
- 'Magic stick' — as in Unit 2, Lesson 6 — Movement awareness (p. 30).
- 'The mermaid of the sea' — as in Unit 2, Lesson 5 — Movement awareness (p. 29).

LESSON 5

Equipment
Counters (hopscotch).

Warm-up
'Jockeys and wild horses' — as in Unit 1, Lesson 2 — Minor games (p. 18).
(T) Emphasize horses galloping.

Skills
- Galloping — forwards, backwards.
(D) One foot leads and the other is brought up quickly to it.
- Make gallops as high as you can.
- With a partner, follow each other's pattern,

e.g. gallop six steps with the same foot leading and swap over.
- Partners make up a sequence involving galloping and other ways of moving. (D)

Application
- Devise various sequences with hopscotch patterns, e.g. hop in every space; hop, jump, hop; hop, miss one, hop; hop, jump backwards, hop.
Have three groups working at once.

  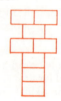

These patterns should ideally be painted on the ground, but tape or chalk would work satisfactorily.

LESSON 6

Equipment
Counters (hopscotch).

Warm-up
'Don't miss out' — children skip, hop, jump, hop, gallop, etc. as directed by teacher around the area. On 'stop' find a partner and bob down, or odd person out, drops out.

Skills/application
Revise as in Unit 3, Lesson 5.
- Introduce hopscotch rules.
1 Throw marker into first square, hop in, pick up marker then hop out backwards. Throw marker into second square, hop into first, second square, pick up marker and hop out backwards and so on.

2 Jump in middle square of first row. Hop into two outside squares of first row. Hop out. Repeat above in second and third squares.

3 Normal hopscotch rules.

PREP ~ GRADE 2

Minor Games

The children will experience running and chasing games, group games and relays, games with equipment, working in group situations.

Helpful hints

- ☐ It is still important to revise boundaries.
- ☐ Use demonstrations to explain games, rather than just verbal instructions.
- ☐ Reinforce honest behaviour and good sportsmanship.
- ☐ It is important that everybody is enjoying the sessions.
- ☐ When choosing teams, try and make them as even in ability as possible.
- ☐ If you find that one team is a lot better or worse than the others, use a handicap system. Give one team a headstart, etc.

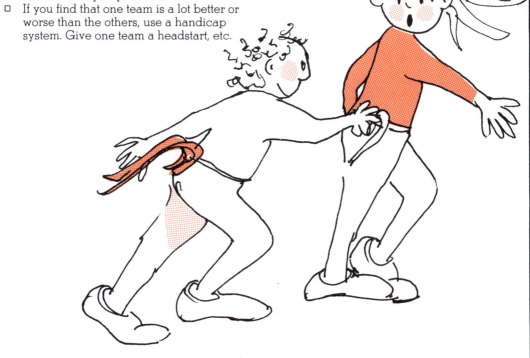

RELATED CLASSROOM ACTIVITIES
General activities relating to specific games

- ☐ Chase the tail (see Lesson 1, p. 44). Discuss the different tails that animals have. Are there any special uses for their tails? Sketches could be drawn of the different tails. Grade them from the smallest to the biggest etc.
- ☐ Concepts of right/left are discussed and developed in class for games. 'Sergeant O'Sullivan' — as in Unit 3, Lesson 5 — Minor games (p. 45).
- ☐ Concepts of on/in are discussed and developed in class for games. 'On the beach, in the sea' — as in Unit 3, Lesson 4 — Minor games (p. 44).

LESSON 1

Equipment
Colour bands (tails), four 20 cm balls.

CHICKEN AND SNAIL
Two coloured balls represent the chicken and the snail. Children make a circle and number one, two, one, two around the circle. Number ones are chickens and number twos snails. Both balls are passed around the circle, the chicken trying to pass the snail.

RELAY BOB BALL
Four lines with a leader in front facing the team. On 'go' he/she passes the ball to the first player who passes it back and bobs down. The ball goes to each player in turn who passes back and bobs down. The last player runs to take the leader's place. The leader becomes number 1 and the game continues.

```
O  O  O  O
x  x  x  x
x  x  x  x
x  x  x  x
x  x  x  x
x  x  x  x
x  x  x  x
```

CHASE THE TAIL
Children tuck colour bands in their belts, skirts, etc. Half the class chase and see how many they can get. Swap over groups.

FARMER JOE AND THE RABBITS
As in Unit 2, Lesson 5 — Minor games (p. 33).

NUMBERS
Three teams of ten players. The teacher calls a number, e.g. 1, 2, 3, etc. and the teams quickly make themselves into that number. The first team to make that number wins.

FROGS IN THE SEA
As in Unit 1, Lesson 3 — Minor games (p. 19).

LESSON 2

Equipment
A tennis ball.

PIRATE'S TREASURE
The pirate sits with eyes closed in the centre of the circle with the treasure (tennis ball) between crossed legs. The teacher points to different children who try to creep up quietly and steal the treasure. The pirate points to where he/she thinks he/she hears a sound. Anyone pointed to goes back. The person who gets back to his/her own place with the treasure becomes the pirate.

DIZZY WHIRL
Make two even teams facing each other. The teams are numbered off starting at opposite ends. When a number is called, one from each side runs to the centre, they join hands and turn each other around until the teacher calls 'dizzy whirl'. They then run back to their places. The first back gets a point for the team. You can call two or three numbers at a time.

IS IT DINNER TIME MR WOLF?
As in Unit 1, Lesson 1 — Minor games (p. 18).

BILLY BOYD
As in Unit 2, Lesson 1 — Minor games (p. 32).

CATCH THE ROBBER (Grades 1, 2)
The children stand in equal parallel lines with hands joined. Two extra children are the policeman and the robber, they run up and down the lines, but cannot go under. At a signal all the players turn right and join hands again. The chase goes in a different direction. Change often.

LESSON 3

Equipment
Four 20 cm balls, one tennis ball.

BILLY BOYD
As in Unit 2, Lesson 1 (p. 32).

CATCH THE ROBBER
As in Unit 3, Lesson 2.

DIZZY WHIRL
As in Unit 3, Lesson 2.

NUMBERS
As in Unit 3, Lesson 1.

CHICKEN AND SNAIL
As in Unit 3, Lesson 1.

RELAY BOB BALL
As in Unit 3, Lesson 1.

PIRATES TREASURE
As in Unit 3, Lesson 2.

LESSON 4

Equipment
A tennis ball.

ON THE BEACH, IN THE SEA
All children stand with their feet on a line. One side of the line is 'on the beach', the other side is 'in the sea'. The teacher calls out 'on the beach' or 'in the sea' and children jump into position. Those who move wrongly are out.

IS IT DINNER TIME MR WOLF?
As in Unit 1, Lesson 1 — Minor games (p. 18).

CRUMBS OR CRUSTS
As in Unit 2, Lesson 1 — Minor games (p. 32).

PIRATE'S TREASURE
As in Unit 3, Lesson 2 (p. 44).

THE SEA AND HER FISH
The teacher is followed by the children. When the teacher says 'the sea is calm' the 'fish' tiptoe. When the teacher says 'the sea is choppy' the fish gallop, and on 'the sea is unhappy' the fish run home with the teacher chasing.

LESSON 5

Equipment
Fifteen to twenty beanbags.

POLICE AND ROBBERS
Divide children into two groups, police and robbers. The police do whatever the teacher/leader says — strip, touch toes, sideways bend, etc. The robbers creep up. When the teacher/leader calls 'charge' the police chase the robbers. Those caught are put into prison.

SERGEANT O'SULLIVAN
Children make four parallel lines. Pick a policeman for each group who watches his/her own group for mistakes. The teacher gives an order, e.g. 'right turn', 'touch toes', etc. If he/she doesn't say 'O'Sullivan says right turn' no one should move. Those who do move are out.

CATCH THE ROBBER
As in Unit 3, Lesson 2 (p. 44).

TOMMY TADDLER
Tommy Taddler stands in an area marked as his ground. The children try to cross his ground saying 'I'm on Tommy Taddler's ground picking up silver and gold! Once on his ground they are not allowed to turn back, but must cross without getting caught. Those caught are put in prison. Variation — place beanbags on ground and the children try to get them without being caught.

ON THE BEACH IN THE SEA
As in Unit 3, Lesson 4 (p. 44).

LESSON 6

Equipment
Fifteen to twenty beanbags, one tennis ball.

ON THE BEACH, IN THE SEA
As in Unit 3, Lesson 4 (p. 44).

TOMMY TADDLER
As in Unit 3, Lesson 5.

SERGEANT O'SULLIVAN
As in Unit 3, Lesson 5.

PIRATE'S TREASURE
As in Unit 3, Lesson 2 (p. 44).

GRADES 3~4
Gymnastics

The children will experience running, jumping, balance, rocking, rolling, weight on hands, partner work and sequences.

Helpful hints

- Emphasize the need for children to sit properly while listening to you — an easy form is 'long sit' where children sit with legs straight out and hands by sides.
- Instead of using the whistle for gymnastics you can use 'and long sit'. Children respond very well to this, especially with some positive reinforcement.
- Always emphasize the need for children to be sensible and to concentrate in gymnastics as accidents can easily happen.
- Take advantage of any child's creativity as they can develop some great ideas.
- Teacher enthusiasm and involvement has a very positive effect on the outcome of the lesson.

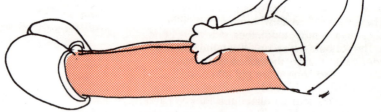

RELATED CLASSROOM ACTIVITIES

Minor theme — locomotion (gymnastics)

- What forms of transport do we use to move ourselves outside the gymnastics room? e.g. bikes, cars, aeroplanes etc.
- What actions do we do to move ourselves in gymnastics? e.g. rocking, rolling, jumping, running.
- Many activities could be centred around the bicycle and the role it plays in our lives, e.g. how a bike works, the different types of bikes, the use of bikes.

Minor theme — ball handling

- Which part of your body moves the ball (Ball Handling) the fastest and the furthest?
- Which would roll further, balloon, football, soccer ball?
- Which action propels the ball further, throwing, rolling, hitting?

Minor theme — warm up (athletics)

- Why do we need to warm-up?
- Why do we stretch muscles?
- What sports do you watch or play where the players warm-up? e.g. football, cricket, racing horses.
- How long do players spend warming-up? e.g. VFL footballer, ballet dancer, jockey, pianist.

Minor theme — fitness (minor games/fitness)

- How much exercise do you do a week? Make a chart to record this.
- How much T.V. do you watch a week? This could be recorded.
- How many hours sleep do you get a week? Make a chart to record this.
- How many hours do you sit each week?
- Many individual and class graphs could be produced to depict the result.

LESSON 1

Equipment
One small gym mat each.

Warm-up
Run forwards, on whistle, hop forwards.
Run and hop, changing direction and signal.
Run with long steps. On whistle, run with short steps.
Jump up making different shapes, e.g. one leg straight and one leg bent, touch your feet.

Skills
- Balancing on one foot and two hands.
- Balancing on any three, four or five body supports.
- Balancing using four body supports and facing up.
- Balancing using three body supports and facing sideways.
- (D) Balancing using five body supports and facing down.
- (D) Rocking in a curled shape, with any body supports.
- (D) Rocking in a wide shape, shoulders and seat as body supports.
- Rolling — thin roll in sideways direction.
- Curled roll in any direction.

(T) Incidentally, check the teaching points for a forward roll — head tucked in, hands shoulder-width apart, look through legs, use hands to push up.
- Weight on hands — move on two hands and two feet facing down, facing up.
- Practise ways of lifting and kicking legs into the air, with weight only on hands.

Application
- Any curled roll → any type of jump.
- A sideways roll → balance using two body supports.

(T) Encourage a smooth sequence and give
(D) demonstrations of different ideas.

LESSON 2

Equipment
A small mat each, and a hoop each.

Warm-up
Run, alternating between stretching tall and bending low.

Run around with hoop doing whatever you like.
Jump over hoop making different shapes.
Jump backwards into hoop in twisted shape.

Skills
- Holding hoop make a bridge shaped **balance**.
- **Balance** on three body supports with your head as the highest part.
- **Balance** inside hoop using two body supports and head facing up.
- **Rolling**, make a wide roll, then a thin roll.
- With a partner make any type of roll through hoop.
- **Weight on hands** — free practice exploring leg shapes in the air, e.g. wide legs before landing, one bent and one straight, legs curled.

Introduce frogstand: sit back on heels, kneel on (T) knees. Place hands in line with knees, lean forward and place head on mat. Raise hips and straighten knees. Place knees one at a time on elbows.

Application
- Perform the following sequence with a (D) partner. Change places with each other with a jump low to the ground → change places with a wide roll → thin roll → change places with a different type of jump.

LESSON 3

Equipment
One cane between two children, a small mat each.

Warm-up
In groups of four to five, 'follow the leader' — (T) showing changes in direction, speed and length of stride. Regularly change leaders by the leader going to the back of the line.
Practise jumping from any take-off but landing on two feet.
With partners, holding a cane — jump over the cane, gradually increasing the height.

Skills
- Roll slowly over cane held by partner.
- Roll quickly under cane held by partner.
- From a standing position perform any curled roll to finish in a standing position.

Throw hands up to finish off roll to help stand up. (T)
Roll from a different starting position (e.g. squat, (D) walking, jumping, running). Roll over cane to a

different finishing position e.g. squat, wide shape on knees, half turn .

- ☐ Weight on hands, explore ways in which the feet land in a different place from where they took off.
- ☐ Revise frogstand.

Application

Ⓓ ☐ With a partner, perform the following sequence. Jump over cane in any shape → own choice of balance → any slow roll to change places with partner. Partner repeats above sequence using different shapes.

LESSON 4

Equipment
A small mat each.

Warm-up
Run, jump, land on one foot and run on.
Run and jump with one leg bent, one leg straight, touching feet with hands. .

Skills
- ☐ With a partner, children explore various balances with their limitations, e.g. one partner on knees, other must have part of the body on the partner and part on the floor; one partner has three body supports, the other has two body supports.
- ☐ Explore rolls in various directions and at various speeds, e.g. thin, fast roll, slow, wide roll.
Ⓣ Introduce straddle roll using the same approach as for forward roll. Legs are then spread wide through roll.
- ☐ With a partner, explore wide rock with/ without contact.
- ☐ Match movements with a partner — wide rock → curled roll → wide rock.
Ⓓ ☐ In contact with partner — wide rock → any roll → wide rock.
- ☐ Weight on hands, any leg shape in air, feet return to same place as for take off.
- ☐ Repeat above, but return feet to a different place.
- ☐ Revise frogstand.

Application
- ☐ With a partner, try a forward roll from a wheelbarrow walk.
Ⓣ Get hips high before rolling over.

LESSON 5

Equipment
A small mat per child.

Warm-up
Run and jump with a wide shape in the air, before landing.
With a partner, run and leapfrog over partner continuously.

Skills
- ☐ Balancing — who can make a 'V sit' by raising their feet up in front of their face?
Arms extend behind back, back leans on 45° Ⓣ angle — not on the ground.
- ☐ What balances can you do with a partner, having no body parts on the ground, e.g.

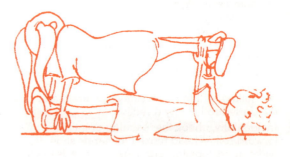

- ☐ Rolling — revise straddle rolls.
- ☐ Try a one-handed forward roll, then try it with Ⓓ no hands.

Application
- ☐ With a partner, perform any slow roll to Ⓓ change places with partner, then any wide jump to change places with partner, then any quick roll to change places with partner.

LESSON 6

Equipment
A small mat each.

Warm-up
Run and squat, place right thumb on ground, run around thumb in one direction, repeat in other direction on the left thumb.
Run and jump making curled shapes in the air.

Skills
- Revise partner balances where whole of body weight is supported by partner.
- 'Echo' balance — partner copies balance demonstrated by partner.
- Introduce backward roll.

Ⓣ Squat and sit on heels. Rock back vigorously, pull hips over head. These first two steps can be practised several times.
Place hands behind shoulders with fingers pointing toward the shoulders; as hips reach point above shoulders push against mat with hands. Feet land on ground to stand up. Partners help each other by supporting back from side view.

Application
Ⓓ
- Sequence — with partner matching — run and jump with one foot take-off → any choice of activity → balance of own choice.
- Run and jump with two foot take-off (to swap places with partner) → slow roll to change places → fast roll to meet with partner.

GRADES 3~4
Ball Handling

The children will experience hitting, rolling, bouncing, throwing, catching, kicking, dribbling.

Helpful hints

- ☐ Let children collect equipment in lines, not all together.
- ☐ Responsibility can be given to children to help hand out equipment — especially those with discipline problems.
- ☐ On whistle, children should immediately stop and place ball between their feet.
- ☐ Give positive reinforcement to those who stop straight away on the whistle, it will encourage the rest of the class.
- ☐ When giving demonstrations, insist that all children are watching.
- ☐ Take advantage of the children's creativity, they come up with some excellent ideas.

LESSON 1

Equipment
A ball each.

Warm-up
'Find a partner' — choose four children to be 'he', who chase the others. Players are not out if they are standing with a partner. You can only stand with another person until the count of three.

Skills
- (D) ☐ Move the ball in any way you like, e.g. hitting, rolling, bouncing, juggling, balancing.
- (D) ☐ Use different parts of your body to move the ball, e.g. hand, foot, elbow, head, nose.
- ☐ How many ways can you move the ball close to the ground?
- ☐ As above, but use different body parts.
- ☐ Move the ball on the spot/about the area. Change on the whistle, use a different body part each time.
- ☐ Standing one metre from your partner, keep the ball close to the ground and pass it to each other.
- ☐ See how many different body parts you can use to pass the ball close to the ground.

Application
- ☐ 'Circle ball' — in groups of eight, children stand with legs apart in a circle. They pass the ball along the ground anywhere in the circle, trying to pass the ball between a person's legs, who defends by using hands only. Variation: use two balls.
- ☐ 'Steal the balls' — double circle formation, one standing with legs astride, the other sitting in leg space, eight balls in centre of circle. On 'go' the crouching players crawl out of legs, run around circle, crawl through legs and into circle to try to get a ball. The balls are put back and players reverse rolls. After ten turns, the pair with the highest score wins.

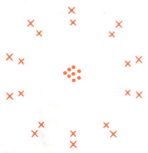

LESSON 2

Equipment
A ball each.

Warm-up
'Jockeys and wild horses' — four jockeys are selected and given a stable in the four corners of the area. Other players gallop around. On 'go' the jockeys catch as many horses as possible leading one to the stable before catching the next. When caught, the horses cannot break away. When all horses are caught, the jockey with the most horses wins.

Skills
- ☐ Use your feet to move the ball. On the whistle change to a different way of moving the ball. (D)
- ☐ Use your hands to keep the ball off the ground. (D)
- ☐ Use your hands, on the whistle, use your feet. Change regularly. (D)

Application
- ☐ 'Eighteen catches' — groups of six stand in circle formation, one ball per group. On 'go', players pass the ball around the circle, when eighteen catches are made without a drop the team sits down. If the ball is dropped, restart count. Variation: repeat as above except stay seated on ground and stand up when finished.
- ☐ 'Beat the runner' — groups of twelve stand in circle formation, one ball per group. The ball is passed across the circle. On 'stop' the player with the ball puts it on the ground and runs around circle. The circle players try to pass the ball around the circle to beat the runner. Variation: see which runner has the least number of passes.

LESSON 3

Equipment
A ball each.

Warm-up
'Train chasey' — in pairs with one player left. Each pair forms a train, the front is the engine and the back the carriage. The odd player tries to attach himself or herself to the back of one of the trains. When attached, the 'engine' of that train has to drop off and attach himself or herself to another train.

Skills

- On the whistle, alternately use hands and feet to move the ball.
- Can you move with the ball held between your feet?
- Can you tap the ball back and forth between your feet? and between your hands?
- Standing one metre from a partner, use different parts of your feet to pass the ball, e.g. toes, heel, side.
- Pass the ball as straight as you can.
- (D) Find different ways of passing the ball using your hands, e.g. bounce, hit, throw.
- Alternately use your hands and then your feet.

Application

- 'Beat the middle' — groups of six to eight in circle formation with one player in the middle and one ball. The circle players pass the ball across the circle, no higher than half a metre above the head of the player in the centre. If caught, the player who threw the ball comes into the centre. If, after ten throws the ball has not been caught, the player with the ball becomes the new person in the centre.

LESSON 4

Equipment
A ball each.

Warm-up
'Find a partner' as in Unit 1, Lesson 1 (p. 51).

Skills

- Use your hands to hit the ball into the air.
- (D) How many other body parts can you use to hit the ball into the air? e.g. elbow, knee, head, foot.
- Move around the area while hitting the ball into the air. Let it bounce once and then catch it.
- Hit the ball as high as you can. Let it bounce twice, then hit it up again.
- (T) Stress that the children should have control over where the ball is going.

Application

- 'Hit me' — groups of five, each group with a ball. One player is 'it'. The other children try to hit 'it' below the knee with the ball. 'It' can defend by hitting the ball with his/her hand.

If hit below the knee, or caught on the full 'it' is out. Take it in turns.

- 'Hit the tail' — the whole class forms a circle with five children in centre holding each other's waists. Outside players throw ball to hit the last person. The leader of the tail is the only one allowed to hit the ball with hands or feet. As the tail is hit, the player joins the circle, until only one is left. The leader of the tail can also go out if he/she hits the ball back to the circle and it is caught on the full.

LESSON 5

Equipment
A ball each.

Warm-up
'Jockeys and wildhorses' as in Unit 1, Lesson 2 (p. 51).

Skills

- Bounce and catch the ball with two hands, one hand.
- Bounce, clap and catch the ball with two hands, one hand.
- Throw the ball above your head, let it bounce, clap and catch it.
- As above, but instead of clapping, turn around, touch the ground and then catch the ball.
- Throw the ball, clap and catch.
- As above, except clap as many times as you can. (D)
- Work out any tricks you can do with the ball. (D)

Application

- 'Dodge the ball' — two teams — one in circle formation the other in free formation in the circle. Team forming the circle throw the ball to hit any of the players below the knee. When a player is hit he/she joins the outside circle. Game may continue until only one player is left or a time limit can be set for each group to see who has the most players left in the circle.
- 'Hit the tail' — as in Unit 1, Lesson 4.

LESSON 6

Equipment
One ball between two children.

Warm-up
'Train chasey' as in Unit 1, Lesson 3 (p. 51).

Skills
- Roll the ball to a partner using two hands, one hand.
- Try and roll the ball straight to your partner.

(T) Step towards your partner with the opposite foot to your throwing hand, bend your back and knees.
- Throw the ball underarm using two hands, one hand.
- Throw the ball overarm using two hands, one hand.
- Bounce the ball to your partner.

(D) See how many other ways you can find of passing the ball to your partner.

Application
- 'Beat the middle' — as in Unit 1, Lesson 3 (p. 52).
- 'Dodge the ball' — as in Unit 1, Lesson 5 (p. 52).

GRADES 3-4
Athletics

The children will experience sprinting — crouch start, hurdling, long jump, running and chasing games, group games.

Helpful hints

- Have all the equipment ready before the lesson starts.
- Picking two monitors to collect the equipment each day works extremely well. Children who need responsibility could be paired with a more responsible child.
- Make sure children are aware of the boundaries for the lesson.
- Give various demonstrations and make sure that all children are watching.
- Try to encourage the children to coach each other and to accept that some children are not as capable as others.
- Do not always allow the children to be with their friends. A good way to do this is to let them find a partner (normally their friend). Then, to make two teams, split the partners.

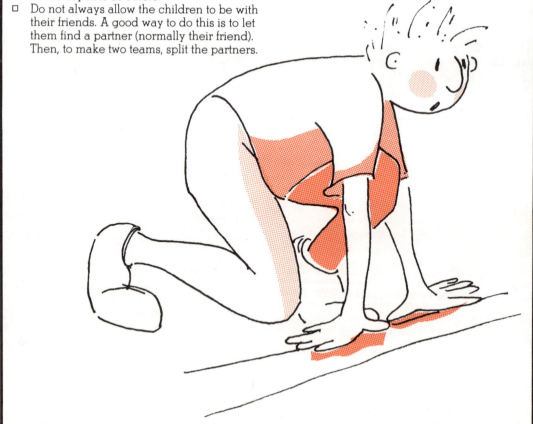

LESSON 1

Equipment
One 20 cm ball.

Warm-up
'Find a partner'. Choose three to four children to be 'he' who chase the others. A player is not out if standing with a partner. They can stay with each other to the count of three.
Stretching — make large and small circles with arms; stretch leg muscles in different directions; kick your leg up high; make circles with your body with feet still.

Skills
- Sprinting — run to the line as fast as you can with your arms straight by your side.
- Repeat above but with your arms behind your back.

(T) Are your arms helping you to run? See if your arms can make you run faster.
Bend slightly forward and bend arms.
Thumb is laid across top of loosely clenched fist.
Swing arms backwards and forth.
Practise running with the correct arm action.
Jog forward and lift knees high.
Jog kicking feet backward to touch bottom.
Which way feels the best and fastest?
Practise sprinting with knees coming up high in front.

Application
- 'Sprinting against catches in a circle' — two teams. Team A sprints a set distance one at a time while team B sees how many catches they can get in a circle in the time. Teams swap over to see who gets the most catches.

LESSON 2

Equipment
One 20 cm ball.

Warm-up
'Fight the bombers' — bombers formed by couples joining inner hands, move freely within the area. Three or four players are fighters and attempt to shoot the bombers by tagging them. When tagged, the bombers must stand and make an archway with hands held overhead. They can be freed to rejoin the game by another bomber flying through their archway. Change fighters regularly.
Stretching — stretch arms back behind head and then forward. Legs astride, bend over and touch opposite arm to leg alternately. Stretch legs by walking forward on hands keeping feet still and then feet up to hands

Skills
- Crouch start

'On your marks' — walk to line, place hands (T)
shoulder-width apart behind line.
Fingers point to the side and thumbs towards the centre.
The knee of the back leg is level with the front foot.
Look at the ground ahead of starting line.
'Set' — lift hips, try and get back horizontal.
Move body weight forward to shoulders.
'Go' — drive body forward, not straight up.
Practise the crouch start with partners.

Application
- 'On your marks, set' — two teams in line formation, 30 metres apart. Each person is numbered as shown. Teacher calls out 'On your marks, set', then a number. The number called run out to see who can get ball first.

1 2 3 4 5 6 7 8 9

●

9 8 7 6 5 4 3 2 1

LESSON 3

Equipment
Hurdles (blocks and canes), one 20 cm ball.

Warm-up
'Group chase' — one person is 'he' and tags others who join on, thus making groups of two, three and four. Groups of four then divide into two couples. The couples continue to chase, tag and divide until there is only one person left.

Stretching — as in Unit 1, Lesson 2.

Skills
- Hurdling — four lanes of three hurdles — walking over hurdles lifting knee high with toe turned up. Pull the trail leg through and out over the hurdle.

- Running over hurdles — practise above action while running.
- Running with knee high — give extra practise to lifting the first knee up high, then pushing down over the hurdle.

Application
- Relays — hurdle down and sprint back to tag the next runner.
- Hurdle the first and crawl under the second and so on.
- 'Hurdling against catches in a circle!' — as in Unit 1, Lesson 1 (p. 55), except team A hurdles instead of sprints.

LESSON 4

Equipment
Hurdles, one 20 cm ball.

Warm-up
'Train chasey' as in Unit 1, Lesson 3 — Ball handling (p. 51).
Stretching — lie on back and move legs as if riding a bike; bend sideways without leaning forward; make large and small circles with arms.

Skills
- Sprinting and hurdling — revise teaching points for sprinting, crouch start, hurdling.
- Relays over hurdles and sprinting back.

Application
- 'Crumbs or crusts' — children in two lines, one metre apart, facing each other. One line is called 'crumbs' the other 'crusts'. The teacher calls out a name, if 'crumbs' is called that line runs away and 'crusts' chase. Any one caught before crossing a given line changes sides.
- 'On your marks, set...' as in Unit 1, Lesson 2 (p. 55).

LESSON 5

Equipment
A small skipping rope each.

Warm-up
'Circles of nine' — children stand in circles of eight, holding hands and a leader in each circle.

On 'go', the players run nine steps to the right, turn and run eight to the left, turn, run seven to the right and so on. On the last step they jump feet together and finish in seated position. The leader counts the running steps out loud.

Skills
- Long jump — run around and jump, taking off with different feet. Find out which way was most comfortable and gave you the longest jump.
- Place a skipping rope on the ground and practise jumping for distance by taking off from the leg you found was most comfortable.
- Run up to your rope at different speeds — slow, medium, fast — which run-up is the best?
- Using the run-up you found best (no more than twenty paces), jump for distance. Also think about gaining height as you jump.

Application
- 'Jumping the creek' — make two lines with ropes for banks of the creek, gradually increasing the width. Children form a line — take a running jump to cross the creek. Variation: children can start where they feel confident and move to the end. Once finished, start at the beginning with a standing long jump.

LESSON 6

Equipment
A small skipping rope each.

Warm-up
'Jockeys and wild horses', as in Unit 1, Lesson 2 — Ball handling (p. 51).

Skills
- Long jump — divide class into two groups, spending equal time at each activity. Practise skills learnt in previous lesson in jumping pit. (If no jumping pit, partners jump against each other.)
- 'Jumping the creek' — as in Unit 1, Lesson 5.

Application
- 'Boats' — groups of five to six players form a file with hands on hips of person in front. On

a signal, the team hops on right legs to a given line and then reverses order and direction to hop back to starting line on left legs.

☐ 'On your marks, set,' as in Unit 1, Lesson 2 (p. 55).

☐ 'Crumbs or crusts', as in Unit 1, Lesson 4 (p. 56).

UNIT 1
GRADES 3-4
Minor Games/Fitness

The children will experience running/chasing games, group games/relays, partner activities, distance running.

Helpful hints
- It is still very important to revise boundaries.
- Use demonstrations to explain activities or games.
- Give positive reinforcement to honest behaviour and good team involvement.
- A quick way to get partners. 'Let's see who's first to find a partner and bob down.'
- Make sure everyone is enjoying the sessions.
- Teacher interest and enthusiasm have a very positive effect on the lesson.
- In hot weather, after a very active lesson, time should be allowed for a quick drink as children dehydrate very easily.

LESSON 1

Equipment
Four canes.

Warm-up
Group chase — one person is 'he' and tags others who join on hands thus making groups of two, three and four. Groups of four then divide into two couples. The couples continue to chase, tag and divide until there is only one person left.

PARTNER ACTIVITIES
- Circle run — one partner stands with one hand up in front of body. The other partner runs around him/her and hits the hand as he/she passes. After five times, partners change places.
- Touch hands — partners stand back to back, bend over and touch hands between their legs and then above their head.
- Through the legs — a partner stands feet astride and one hand out. The other partner runs behind and through the legs, stands and hits his/her partner's hand. Change places every five turns.

RELAYS IN TEAMS OF SIX
- Touch the line — one at a time, run to touch line and back.
- Jump the stick — the first person runs with cane to touch the line and return to run down the side of the team holding the stick low to the ground. As he/she passes, each team member jumps over the cane. Pass it on to number two.
- Carry your toes — the first person takes hold of their toes and hops to line and sprints back.
- Trains — the first person runs up to line forwards and returns backwards. He/she picks up the next person and takes him/her up to the line and runs backwards to pick up the next person and so on.

GAME
- Train chasey as in Unit 1, Lesson 3 — Ball handling (p. 51).

LESSON 2

Equipment
Twelve bean bags, eight canes.

Warm-up
Chase the beanbag — twelve children hold a beanbag. A person is 'he' and tries to tag a player in possession of a beanbag. If successful a new chaser is chosen. Children should be encouraged to run and dodge, but if capture is certain, throw a beanbag to another player.

PARTNER ACTIVITIES
- Circle run — as in Unit 1, Lesson 1.
- Side to side — partners stand back to back with arms sideways. They clasp hands and bend from side to side to touch knees.
- Leapfrog — partner A stands in a bent position for partner B to leapfrog over. Change after five jumps.
- Touch hands — as in Unit 1, Lesson 1.

RELAYS
- Jump the stick — as in Unit 1, Lesson 1.
- Back to front relay — the first player runs from rear of team, up to line, down the side of team, around rear of team to the front. The first player then takes the team up to line and back. The next player is the person at the back. Variation: skip, hop, jump.
- Trains — as in Unit 1, Lesson 1.

GAME
- Cars — players are given names of cars, coinciding in each team. When leader calls out a car name the player from each team runs to the line and back. First back scores a point for their team. On 'all cars' all players one at a time starting from back crawl through legs of those in front, run to line and back. First team with a straight line wins a point.

LESSON 3

Equipment
Nil.

Warm-up
Fight the bombers — bombers formed by couples joining inner hands, move freely within the area. Three to four players are fighters and attempt to shoot the bombers by tagging them. When tagged, the bombers must stand and make an archway with hands held overhead. They can be freed to rejoin the game by another bomber flying through their archway. Change fighters regularly.

PARTNER ACTIVITIES
- Leapfrog — as in Unit 1, Lesson 2 (p. 59).
- Side to side — as in Unit 1, Lesson 2 (p. 59)
- Partner standing — partners sit back to back with knees bent and arms interlocked. Try and stand up together whilst backs remain in contact. Try again from sitting to standing position.
- Hopping bumps — partners hold up one leg and place their other hand behind their back. They then bump each other until one is forced to place to other foot on the ground.

GAMES
- Cats and mice — circle formation. Select two children to stand inside circle (mice) and two outside (cats). The cats chase the mice ducking under arms but not breaking arms. Circle tries to help the mice.
- Through the legs — children in groups of three to four run freely within area. On whistle, the leader of each team stands with legs wide while other team members run to crawl through leader's legs. As each member passes he stands up, legs wide, thereby extending tunnel for others to crawl through. The first team to line up scores a point. On whistle, leader crawls through legs followed by rest of team until all members are running again.
- Cars — as Unit 1, Lesson 2 (p. 59).

LESSON 4

Equipment
Five balls at two corners of school.

Warm-up
Group chase — as in Unit 1, Lesson 1 (p. 59).

PARTNER ACTIVITIES
- Partner run — partner A stands on one side of centre line and partner B on the other. On 'go', A runs to respective side line and returns to touch B's hand. B then runs to line and back to A. See how many times partners touch hands in 60 seconds.
- Hopping bumps as in Unit 1, Lesson 3.
- Partner standing — as in Unit 1, Lesson 3.
- Partner cars — partners face each other with hands on shoulders. Partner A moves backwards while B steers. On signal, reverse order.

DISTANCE RUNS
- Children run around school boundary with the following variations. a Walk for 40 steps, run for 40 steps. b Run to corner — throw and catch ball ten times; touch toes ten times; bounce and catch ball ten times; do ten sit ups.

Send children off at different time intervals. They (T) do as many laps as they can.

GAMES
- Boats — groups of four players form a file with hands on hips of person in front. On a signal the team hops on right legs to line and then reverses order and direction to hop back to starting line on left legs.

LESSON 5

Equipment
Nil.

Warm-up
Dog and cat — form a double circle facing centre and paired off, as shown in diagram. One pair is selected as being the dog, and the other the cat. The dog has to chase the cat and the cat plays safe by standing behind a pair. This makes the front player the next cat and the game continues. Encourage 'cats' to change all the time. (T)

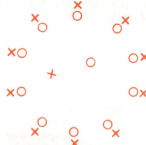

PARTNER ACTIVITIES
- Hand jump — partner A holds hand high, from a standing position B jumps up to touch A's hand with his/her head. If successful, repeat from a crouch position. A may need to stand on toes.
- Partner cars — as in Unit 1, Lesson 4.
- Partner run — as in Unit 1, Lesson 4.
- Knee chasey — partner A is chased by B until B can touch A behind the knee. The roles are changed every thirty seconds. Stay in a three metre square.

GAMES

☐ One versus three — groups of four, numbers one to three join hands to make a triangle. A fourth person tries to touch in anyway possible the number three person in the triangle. When successful, he/she changes places with number three and the game starts again.

☐ Through the legs — as in Unit 1, Lesson 3 (p. 60).

☐ Boats — as in Unit 1, Lesson 4 (p. 60).

LESSON 6

Equipment
Two 20 cm balls.

Warm-up
Fight the bombers — as in Unit 1, Lesson 3 (p. 59).
Sideways slipping — partners stand back to back, arms interlocked. From the line they move sideways with side slipping to line and back. Repeat several times.
Hand jump — as in Unit 1, Lesson 5 (p. 60).
Knee chasey — as in Unit 1, Lesson 5 (p. 60).
Hopping wrestle — partners stand on one foot and hold opponent's hand. With hopping and pulling movements each partner tries to unbalance the other.

DISTANCE RUNS
Children divide into groups of eight and follow the leader around the school boundary. Swap leaders at each corner.

GAMES

☐ Dodge the ball — the class is divided into two teams, one in circle formation, the other in free formation in the circle. Team forming the circle throws the ball to hit any of the players below the knee. When a player is hit he/she joins the circle. Game may continue until only one player is left, or a time limit can be set for each group to see who has the most players left in the circle. Variation: use two balls at once.

UNIT 2

GRADES 3~4
Gymnastics

The children will experience jumping — scissor jump; balancing — individual, with partners; rocking, rolling; sequences — groups, with small equipment.

Helpful hints
- Revise 'long-sit' as a proper way to sit and listen in gymnastics.
- This unit particularly allows for the child's creativity, so take advantage of it.
- This unit allows you to give the less skilled child individual goals to aim for.
- Try to encourage the children to coach each other.
- When working in groups for sequences, don't always let children be with their friends, as this allows for children to learn from each other.
- Reward and encourage 'triers'.
- Make sure you enjoy the session as much as the children.

RELATED CLASSROOM ACTIVITIES

Minor theme — Locomotion
- Which types of animals can move in a similar way to us?
- Which animals can run? Which are the fastest?
- Which animals can jump?
- Which animals move in different ways from us, e.g. snake, fish, bird, platypus.

Minor theme — Fitness
- What are the good foods that we should eat everyday?
- Lists and charts could be made of the five main food groups of good and bad food the children eat.
- Children could record what they eat for a day/week.
- Many graphs could be produced to depict the results.

Minor theme — Athletics
- Which competition athletic events are there in your area?
- Make a list of all the athletic events you can think of.
- Order all the athletic events into different skill areas, e.g. running — sprints, long distance, relays. Throwing — shot-put, discus. Jumping — long, high, triple jump.

Minor theme — Games
- Children analyse various games they are involved in, or familiar with, in terms of the skills used, e.g. football — kicking, catching, bouncing, etc.
- Various groups could analyse different sports.

LESSON 1

Equipment
A small gym mat each.

Warm-up
Run and jump, making a curled shape in the air before landing.
Run, jump, land on one foot and run on.

Skills
- Balance on three body supports, then move into a curled roll, return to same balance.
- With a partner, one person balances with part of his/her body on partner and part on the ground.
- Roll in different directions — forwards, backwards, sideways.
- Roll at fast, medium, slow speeds.
- Sequence — roll in one direction, then roll in a different direction and at a different speed.

Application
- Mirror balance with partner, change places with curled roll and balance again.
- Group balance in fours, any type of roll away from group, individual balance, any type of roll back to group, group balance as first used.

LESSON 2

Equipment
Six hoops, six ropes, six blocks and canes, a small gym mat each.

Warm-up
'Follow the leader' — in groups of five run and jump over equipment spread around playground.
Ⓣ Encourage moving in different ways, speeds, directions. Change leaders regularly. Use six hoops, six ropes, six canes and blocks.

Skills
- Partners rock without making contact with each other.
- Ⓓ ▫ Match movements with partner, e.g. wide rock → curled roll → wide rock.
- Ⓣ Emphasize quality in movement.
- Rolling in a forward direction with any finishing position, e.g. stand, squat, half turn.
- Ⓓ Demonstrate forward roll → any type of jump.

Application
- In groups of four, using any equipment used Ⓓ initially (hoops, ropes, canes and blocks) develop a group sequence to include: any type of jump → any type of rock → any type of roll → balance.

LESSON 3

Equipment
Small skipping rope between three, a small gym mat each.

Warm-up
In groups of three with a rope, run and jump over rope, gradually increasing height.
Run and jump making various shapes before Ⓓ landing.
Jump over rope from a standing position, gradually increasing height.

Skills
- With weight on hands, make any leg shape in air, feet down in same place as take-off.
- Weight on hands, feet down in a different place from take-off.
- With a partner, rock so as to make contact with each other.
Encourage and demonstrate different ways of Ⓣ making contact.
- Sequence — wide rock → any roll → wide Ⓓ rock in contact with partner.

Application
- Partner sequence — children use ropes if Ⓓ they wish. **Rock** (with partner) → **roll** away from partner → **weight on hands** back to partner → partner **balance**.

LESSON 4

Equipment
One cane between two. A small gym mat each.

Warm-up
Run, gradually increasing and decreasing speed.
With a partner and one cane — jump over cane, gradually increasing height; jump half twist → jump half twist over cane.

Skills

- Scissor kick over cane held by partner.

(T) Hold cane at knee height, approach at angle almost parallel to it, lift side leg high and over cane, as leading leg comes down, lift the other leg.

(D)
- Revise V sit (Unit 1) i.e. make a V by raising feet in front of face.
- Partner balance — partner A on hands and feet, B with part of body on partner and part on ground.
- Partner A in wide shape and B in curled shape.

(D)
- Partner A with four body supports and B with none.
- In pairs one holds cane, other rolls under cane, then over it.

Application

(D)
- Any type of roll under cane → jump → any type roll over cane.

LESSON 5

Equipment
A small gym mat each, one hoop between two.

Warm-up
Run and leap (one foot take-off), land, run on.
Run and jump (two foot take-off), land, run on.
With a partner holding a hoop, run and jump into hoop, run and jump over hoop.

Skills

- Sequence of three rolls, changing direction and speed.
- With a partner holding a hoop, roll through hoop.
- In pairs, partner A balances on five body supports, B on three body supports.
- Partner A balances with feet as the highest part of balance.

(D)
- Partner A balances with no body supports.

Application

(D)
- Partner sequence (with or without hoop) — weight on hands → series of quick rolls, weight on hands → any type of roll → balance.

LESSON 6

Equipment
A small gym mat each, ten canes, ten hoops, ten balls.

Warm-up
Run and jump (one foot take-off) → own choice of activity.
Run and jump (two foot take-off) → own choice of activity.

Skills/Application

- In pairs, using any equipment, compose a sequence of balance → roll → weight on hands → balance.
- Groups of six, using any equipment, compose a sequence of weight on hands activity → any type of roll → any type of balance. (D)

GRADES 3~4
Ball Handling

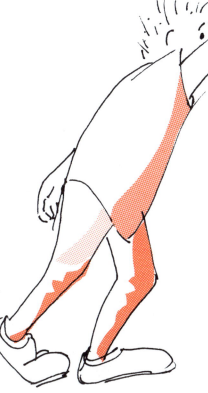

The children will experience rolling, stopping, kicking, bouncing, throwing, catching.

Helpful hints

- Whistle means stop, listen and ball between feet.
- A less skilled child can be partnered by a more proficient child without too much fuss.
- Have a demonstration prepared while the rest of the class are involved in an activity.
- A quick way to pick two teams — let the children bob down with a partner, then one goes to team A and the other to team B.
- Colour bands are useful to distinguish teams.
- Have equipment ready (balls pumped up) before lesson starts.
- Responsibility can be given to children to be equipment monitors — partnering a discipline problem with a responsible child can often bring positive results.
- Are the children happy and healthy?

LESSON 1

Equipment
One ball between two.

Warm-up
'Chase the ball' — twelve children hold a ball. A person is 'he' and tries to tag a player in possession of a ball. If successful a new chaser is chosen. Children should be encouraged to run and dodge, but if capture is certain, throw the ball to another player.

Skills
- In pairs, find different ways of passing the ball, e.g. roll, kick, push, bounce, throw, hit etc.
- Try and use many body parts to pass the ball.
- Pass the ball at various heights — in the air, along the ground.
- Pass the ball straight to your partner — in the air, along the ground.
- Pass the ball so your partner has to move to stop it — in the air, along the ground.
- Standing 1 metre apart, pass the ball. Every time it is caught take one step back. When it is dropped, take one step in.

Application
- Continuous two ball — divide class in half on court. One at a time children hit the ball into opponents' half and run to end of their line. If ball is missed or not returned the player drops out, until one person is left.

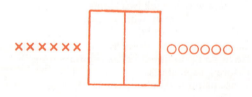

LESSON 2

Equipment
One ball between two.

Warm-up
'Fight the bombers' — bombers formed by couples joining inner hands, move within area. Three to four players are fighters and attempt to shoot the bombers by tagging them. When tagged, they stand and make an archway with hands held overhead. They can be freed to rejoin the game by another bomber flying through their archway. Change fighters regularly.

Skills
- In pairs, find how many different ways you can stop the ball.
- Pass the ball so your partner has to move to stop the ball.
- Both partners move while passing and stopping the ball.
- Children practise their best way of passing and stopping the ball.

Application
- 'Beat the middle' — groups of six to eight form circles with one player in centre. The circle players pass the ball across the circle, no higher than half a metre above the head of the player in the centre. If caught, the player who threw the ball comes into the centre. If, after ten throws, the ball has not been caught, the player with the ball goes into the centre.

LESSON 3

Equipment
One ball between two. One block between two.

Warm-up
'Boats' — players form a file with hands on hips of person in front. On a signal, the teams hop on right legs to line and then reverse order and direction to hop back to starting line on left legs.

Skills
- In pairs, free activity with ball.
- Pass the ball in as many different ways as you can using your hands.
Step forward with opposite foot to throwing hand. Follow hand through in direction of pass. Try and pass the ball straight to your partner.
- One block between two children as they try to hit the block in various ways.

Application
- 'Guard the block' — groups of six, two balls and one block per group. The players form a circle around the block in the centre. The block is guarded by a player who uses hands or feet to deflect or stop balls thrown at the

block. Any player who hits the block changes places with the defender. Variations: use two balls.

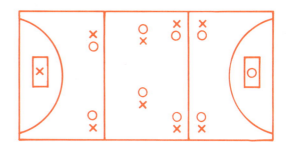

LESSON 4

Equipment
One ball between two, one hoop between two.

Warm-up
'One versus three' — groups of three, numbered one to three join hands to make a triangle. A fourth person tries to touch in any way possible the number three person in the triangle. When successful he/she changes places with number three and the game starts again.

Skills
- ☐ With a partner, catch the ball in as many ways as you can, e.g. one or two hands, low, high, medium.
- ☐ Bounce the ball and catch it in different ways.
- ☐ Using a hoop, find ways of passing the ball to your partner, e.g. bounce in hoop, pass through hoop, roll through hoop, kick through hoop.

Application
- ☐ 'Name ball' — groups of eight, one ball each group. One player throws ball in air and calls name of a player in the circle. If player catches it he/she throws it up and calls another name. If dropped, the player has to run after it and call 'stop' when he/she has it. He/she then throws it to try to hit someone, who, if hit, becomes the next person to throw the ball and call someone's name.

LESSON 5

Equipment
Two small gym mats, one 20 cm ball, colour bands.

Skills/Application
HIT THE MAT
- ☐ Two even teams positioned as in diagram, i.e. equal numbers in each third of the netball court.
- ☐ Children only allowed to play in their third of the court.
- ☐ No-one allowed in the goal circle except person on mat (place mat towards top of circle).
- ☐ Players are rotated every five minutes from one third to the next.
- ☐ The ball is thrown up between two centre players. Each team passes the ball until it can be thrown to the catcher with a clear pass. This scores one point for the team. The ball then returns to the centre for a throw-up.
- ☐ The ball must be caught in each third.
- ☐ No running with the ball.
- ☐ Defenders must stand 1 metre away from their opponents.
- ☐ You can hold the ball for 3 seconds.
- ☐ No body contact is allowed.
- ☐ If any rules are violated a free pass is given to the opposing team at the same spot.

Encourage and give positive reinforcement to good team effort and fair play.

LESSON 6

Equipment
Two small gym mats, one 20 cm ball, colour bands.

Skills/Application
- ☐ 'Hit the mat' — as in Unit 2, Lesson 5.

GRADES 3~4
Athletics

The children will experience walking, shuttle relay, shot put.

Helpful hints
- Always encourage children to do their very best.
- Always emphasize safety aspects, especially when using such equipment as the shot.
- Give demonstrations so children are able to see the correct technique.
- Both children and teacher can be used to give demonstrations.
- Give the less skilled child individual goals to aim for.
- Make it known if a child has improved
- In hot weather especially, time should be allowed at the end of the lesson for a quick drink — children dehydrate very easily.

LESSON 1

Equipment
One ball.

Warm-up
'Walking tag' — two to three players are 'it'. The remaining players are chased and tagged by walking. Players are safe if standing on one leg with the right arm under the right thigh and holding the nose.
Stretching — stretch various parts of the body.

Skills
□ Walk in straight line.
□ Walk in curved lines.
Ⓣ Teaching points for walking:
Feet — point forward, heel is the first part of the foot to touch ground. The back foot does not move until the front foot touches the ground, as heel touches the ground the knee locks (straightens).
Arms — bent at an angle less than 90°. Swing arms forward and across body, arms should be relaxed.
Head — eyes looking in direction you are going, not downwards.

Application
□ 'Walking against catches in a circle' — class is divided into equal teams. Team 1 walks a certain distance one at a time. Team 2 sees how many catches they can get in a circle in the time it takes Team 1 to walk. Teams swap over to see who can get the most throws.

LESSON 2

Equipment
Nil.

Warm-up
'Here, there and nowhere' — children listen to teacher. On 'here' children walk quickly in direction indicated by teacher. On 'there' children follow direction again. On 'nowhere' children walk on the spot.
Stretching — a child is selected to stretch arm and leg muscles.

Skills
Ⓣ Revise teaching points for walking as in Unit 2, Lesson 1.

Teaching points for hip action: Ⓣ
Stand with feet together, alternately bend each leg so the hips rotate.
Walk and make sure foot lands heel first, the knee straightens and remains so until the other leg swings through and lands.
□ With a partner, one person walks while the other watches and gives advice.

Application
□ 'Cowboys and horses' — cowboys sit with legs crossed, facing the centre of the circle. The horses stand behind the cowboy with legs astride. Teacher either calls (i) cowboys — who crawl through horses' legs, walk around circle and back through legs; (ii) horses walk around circle and back to place. Change over positions regularly.

LESSON 3

Equipment
One baton between two; one ball.

Warm-up
'Find a partner' — choose three to four children to be 'he' who chase the others. A player is not out if standing with a partner. They can stay with each other to the count of three.
Stretching — select three children each to give a warm-up stretch.

Skills
Introduce teaching points for passing baton for   Ⓣ
shuttle relay:
Keep eyes on the person you are giving it to.
Hold the bottom of the baton.
Pass to receiver at top speed.
□ Practise passing baton to partner — standing still, walking, then running.
Teaching points for receiving baton: Ⓣ
Eyes on baton.
Reach forward, but be relaxed.
Make a semi-circle with both hands, thumbs in and fingers out.
Hands are held at shoulder height.
Hands close over baton.
Adjust grip when running to have one hand at the bottom of the baton.
□ Practise passing and receiving baton with a partner — slowly at first and gradually increasing speed.

Application

- Shuttle relay — divide class into groups of eight. Run to centre, place baton down, run on and tag next runner, who picks up baton and passes it on to next runner and so on.

Variations: walk, hop, skip, jump.
- Shuttle relay versus catches in a circle. — as in Unit 2, Lesson 1 (p. 69) except a shuttle relay is completed rather than walking.

LESSON 4

Equipment
One baton between two; one 20 cm ball.

Warm-up
Walking tag — as in Unit 2, Lesson 1 (p. 69). Stretching — select three different children to demonstrate stretches and to explain why they are doing them.

Skills
- Walking and shuttle relay — revise and practise walking technique as in Unit 2, Lessons 1 and 2 (p. 69). Revise passing and receiving batons with partners.

Application
- Walking shuttle relay — as in Unit 2, Lesson 3, except baton is passed to next person rather than placed on ground.
- Chase the baton — eight batons are handed to children. Three to four children are 'he' who chase children with a baton in their hand. If caught with a baton in hand, children drop out until no-one is left. Children being chased attempt to pass baton on to someone else.
- Shuttle relay versus catches in a circle — as in Unit 2, Lesson 3.

LESSON 5

Equipment
Shots, softballs, tennis balls (if needed).

Warm-up
'Here, there and nowhere' — as in Unit 2 Lesson 2 (p. 69).
Stretching — three different children are selected to lead stretches and to explain why they are doing them.

Skills
Everyone has a ball (rotate shot-puts so everyone has a turn).
- Introduce the skill of throwing the shot.

Holding the shot — place shot on four fingers and support with thumb. The shot is placed against the neck and under the chin with the elbow out at the side. Stand side on to the direction of throw. Raise your other arm to balance you.

Releasing the shot — step back and bend down on the right leg. As the body rises turn to face forwards. Push the shot and extend the arm to drive it out. Extend the fingers to give a final push.
- Children practise individually with the emphasis on correct technique. For safety reasons all children throw at once, then when teacher signals, all go and collect together.

Application
- Bowl the shot — in groups of four, children aim to get as close to the target as possible. The closest person each time scores a point. 'Challenge' amongst winners.

LESSON 6

Equipment
Shots, soft balls, tennis balls, four batons, one 20 cm ball.

Warm-up
Find a partner — as in Unit 2, Lesson 3 (p. 69).
Stretching — as in Unit 2, Lesson 5.

Skills
- Revise skills for shot-put taught in Unit 2, Lesson 5.

Application
- Bowl the shot — as in Unit 2 Lesson 5.
- Shuttle relay versus catches in a cirlce — as in Unit 2, Lesson 3.
- Cowboys and horses — as in Unit 2, Lesson 2 (p. 69).

GRADES 3~4

Minor Games/Fitness

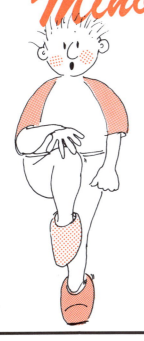

The children will experience partner activities, relays, group games, skipping (long rope),

Helpful hints

- ☐ Try to develop an attitude of fair play amongst all children.
- ☐ Try to help children to accept that everyone has different abilities.
- ☐ Keep children working hard — it is good for them to be puffing at the end.
- ☐ After active sessions, children are going to need a drink at the conclusion of the lesson.
- ☐ Have demonstrations ready and correct for the children to see.
- ☐ Games are a good opportunity for children to help coach each other.
- ☐ Are the children active and energetic?

LESSON 1

Equipment
Two 20 cm balls.

Warm-up
Jog on spot holding hands at waist level, bring knees up to touch hands.

Run making various ground patterns such as circles, squares, zig-zags.

Crumbs or crusts — children stand in two lines facing each other, one metre apart. One line is called 'crumbs' and the other 'crusts'. The teacher calls 'crumbs' or 'crusts' and the line called runs away pursued by the other line. If caught they join that line.

PARTNER ACTIVITIES
- ☐ Circle run — partner A stands with hand up. Partner B runs around and hits the hand as he/she passes. After five times change positions.
- ☐ Touch hands — partners stand back to back and bend over and touch hands between their legs and then above their head.
- ☐ Knee chasey — partner A is chased by partner B until B can touch A behind the knee on the lower leg. Roles are changed every 30 seconds.
- ☐ Side to side — stand back to back. With arms sideways partners clasp hands and bend from side to side to touch their knees.

RELAYS
- ☐ Jump the river relay — number 1 runs behind the team and jumps over legs and back to his/her place. Number 2 continues and so on.
- ☐ Carry your toes — hold onto your toes, hop up to line and sprint back.

GAME
- ☐ Dodge the ball — one team stands in circle formation, the other in free formation in the circle. Team forming the circle throws the

ball (use two balls to hit any players below the knee. When hit, you join the outside circle. Play until no-one is left or to a time limit.

LESSON 2

Equipment
Four balls, five beanbags.

Warm-up
'Fight the bombers' — as in Unit 1, Lesson 3 (p. 59).

PARTNER ACTIVITIES
- Partner run — partner A stands on one side of centre line and B on the other. On 'go' A runs to respective side line and returns to touch B's hand. B then runs to line and back to A. See how many times partners can touch in 60 seconds. Variations: hop, skip.
- Knee chasey — as in Unit 2, Lesson 1.
- Touch hands — as in Unit 2, Lesson 1.
- Partner twist — stand face to face with hands together. Rotate hands, arms and body while still holding on. Rotate back again.

RELAYS
- First and last relay — on 'first', team members run around leader, on 'last' the team runs around the end person.
- Jump the river relay — as in Unit 2, Lesson 1.

- Overhead relay — number one passes the ball overhead to number two and so on to the

end of the line. The end person sprints to the line and returns to the start of the line by rolling the ball. The ball is then passed overhead as before.
- Carry your toes — as in Unit 2, Lesson 1.

GAMES
- Leapfrog the circle — the group of six to eight, stands in a circle with everyone in leapfrog position. One person leapfrogs around the circle and back to starting position. As soon as the first person jumps over the second, this person also starts leapfrogging around the circle. Variation: leapfrog over first person, crawl through legs of second person.

LESSON 3

Equipment
A large skipping rope.

Warm-up
'Continuous tiggy' — four players are 'he'. They tag as many players as they can. When caught, the player joins hands and so on until no-one is left.

PARTNER ACTIVITIES
- Hop and pull — partners face each other, grasp left hands and their own raised left ankle with right hands. Each tries to pull their partner off balance with hopping and pulling movements.
- Partner twist — as in Unit 2, Lesson 2 (p. 72).
- Partner run — as in Unit 2, Lesson 2 (p. 72).
- Wheelbarrow walk — partner A places his/her hands on the ground. Partner B grasps A's ankles, or just above the knees, and walks along.

SKIPPING ACTIVITIES (with a large rope)
- Run through loop, miss one loop → no misses.
- Run through with partners, miss one → no misses. Drop out if you miss a turn.
- Run in, jump one and then out and miss one → no misses.
- Partners as above — drop out if a loop is missed.

GAME

- Cats and mice — select two children to stand inside circle (mice) and two outside (cats). The cats chase the mice ducking under arms, but not breaking arms. Circle tries to help the mice.

LESSON 4

Equipment
A long skipping rope.

Warm-up
'Crumbs and crusts' — as in Unit 2, Lesson 1 (p. 72).

PARTNER ACTIVITIES

- Through the legs — partner A stands feet astride with one hand out. The other partner runs behind and through the legs, stands up and hits his/her partner's hand. Change places every five turns.
- Wheelbarrow walk — as in Unit 2, Lesson 3.
- Hop and pull — as in Unit 2, Lesson 3.
- Partner cars — partners face each other with hands on each other's shoulders. Partner A trots backwards while B steers. On signal reverse order.

SKIPPING ACTIVITIES (with a long rope)

- Run through rope — single, miss one, no misses, with a partner.
- See how many times you can run through without a miss (or depending on the skill level with one miss).
- As above, except run in and jump one.

GAMES

- Cats and mice — as in Unit 2, Lesson 3.
- Leapfrog the circle — as in Unit 2, Lesson 2 (p. 72).

LESSON 5

Equipment
A large skipping rope, two 20 cm balls.

Warm-up
'Hunters and hares' — two children are the hunters and have a ball each. The rest (the hares) line up behind the line. Each hunter in turn decides how the hares will move to the next line, e.g. run, hop, walk, crawl, etc. The two hunters perform the same movement and attempt to hit the hares with the balls. When hit, the hares remain where they are and become poisonous trees. This means they can reach with their hands and tag any hares that come near the tree. Each time the hares make it safely to the end line a new movement is called.

SKIPPING

- As in Unit 2, Lesson 4. Depending on the skill attempt 'alphabet skip'. One person at a time jumps in for one and then out with the following rhyme.
  1st   A
  2nd   word that begins with A, e.g. apple
  3rd   B
  4th   word that begins with B, e.g. banana,
  and so on.

GAME

- Dodge the ball — as in Unit 2, Lesson 1 (p. 72).

LESSON 6

Equipment
Four balls.

Warm-up
'Continuous tiggy' — as in Unit 2, Lesson 3 (p. 73).

RELAYS

- Jump the river relay — as in Unit 2, Lesson 1 (p. 72).
- Carry your toes — as in Unit 2, Lesson 1 (p. 72).
- Overhead relay — as in Unit 2, Lesson 2 (p. 72).
- First and last relay — as in Unit 2, Lesson 2 (p. 72).

SKIPPING

- Boys and girls competition — run through rope on your own, with a partner. See who can run through the most times. Run in and jump one, on your own, with a partner.

GAMES

- Dodge the ball — as in Unit 2, Lesson 1 (p. 72).
- Leapfrog the circle — as in Unit 2, Lesson 2 (p. 72).
- Cats and Mice — as in Unit 2, Lesson 3 (p. 73).

GRADES 3~4
Gymnastics

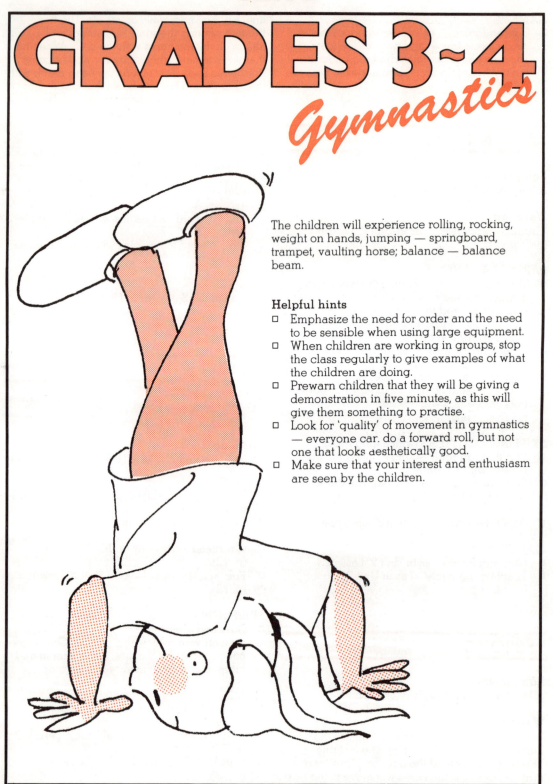

The children will experience rolling, rocking, weight on hands, jumping — springboard, trampet, vaulting horse; balance — balance beam.

Helpful hints

- Emphasize the need for order and the need to be sensible when using large equipment.
- When children are working in groups, stop the class regularly to give examples of what the children are doing.
- Prewarn children that they will be giving a demonstration in five minutes, as this will give them something to practise.
- Look for 'quality' of movement in gymnastics — everyone car. do a forward roll, but not one that looks aesthetically good.
- Make sure that your interest and enthusiasm are seen by the children.

RELATED CLASSROOM ACTIVITIES

Minor theme — locomotion (gymnastics)

☐ Circus animals can be looked at in terms of how they move, e.g. which animals do balancing acts? which animals do jumping acts? which animals do running acts? What other gymnastic activities are there at the circus?

Minor theme — games (ball handling)

☐ Children can explore all the different hitting implements used in games, e.g. bats — softball, bat-tennis, cricket; sticks — hockey, croquet, polo; racquets — tennis, badminton, squash.

☐ Groups of children could investigate the different types of hitting games — similarities, differences, etc. could be compared and graphed.

Minor theme — athletics at the Olympics (athletics)

☐ What athletic events are there in the Olympics?

☐ Who are some famous Australian athletes?

☐ Pretend you are an athlete at the Olympics. What would it feel like before the event? After winning a gold medal?

☐ Children in partners/small groups could revise with each other the 'teaching points' for various athletic events. This could be in practical or written form.

Minor theme — fitness (minor games/fitness)

☐ Set children a task to begin a simple change in their life to improve their health/fitness, e.g. eat fruit instead of buying lollies at lunch time; only buy your lunch once a week; instead of watching T.V. after school, do something outside or with a friend; get ten hours sleep, six nights a week; go for a run at school at lunchtime. Children should keep a diary and record anything relevant.

LESSON 1

Equipment

A hoop each, trampet, gym mat (half the grade).

Warm-up

With one hoop each, children move around the area bowling the hoop at varying speeds. Jump in and out of hoop in various ways.

Skills/Application

In these two activities the groups can rotate at half time.

1 Jumping, using trampet with teacher supervision.

Revise basic technique for using the trampet:
Take off from one foot to land on trampet. ⓣ
Take off from two feet to jump off trampet.
Jump up and not forward.
Jump making various shapes in the air — wide, curled.
Jump making a half turn in the air.
Jump making a full turn in the air.

2 Rocking, rolling and balancing — children in groups of four develop the following sequence: any type of rock → roll in any direction → any type of rock → any type of balance. Hoops can be used in any part of the sequence.

Encourage children to practise sequence aiming ⓣ at perfect flow and movement.

LESSON 2

Equipment

A small skipping rope each, a gym mat between two children, trampet, large mat.

Warm-up

Each child has a skipping rope — allow free exploration, on the spot/while moving.

Skills

☐ Introduce the headstand.

Sit on heels with hands in line with knees. Lean ⓣ forward to put head on mat. Lift hips by walking feet in as far as you can. Lift legs until straight and back slightly arched. Practise with partner, one spotting at side.

Application

Two groups should rotate between the following activities:
1 Jumping on trampet (with teacher supervision).

(T) Introduce tuck jump. Bounce upwards, while in the air tuck your heels up to your bottom. Shoulders should be level with hips, not forward.
2 Weight on hands — partners practise headstands — one as spotter, supporting back and standing at side of partner, so you don't get kicked.
(D) □ Change places with partner with weight on hands activity, followed by a roll, then a balance.

LESSON 3

Equipment

Trampet, large mat, small mat between two children, canes.

Warm-up

Run around the area and spring into the air. Run with long, then small steps. Jump in the air making different shapes.

Skills

□ Weight on hands — introduce the cartwheel. Let a child demonstrate if he/she is doing it correctly.
(T) Hands and feet all land in one line. Arms, put down strongly, legs, kick up strongly. Keep elbows straight. Push from ground to help stand up.

Application

Rotate between the following two activities.
1 Jumping on trampet (with teacher supervision). Revise tuck jump, as in Unit 3, Lesson 2. Tuck jump over a cane held by teacher. Increase the height depending on the ability of the children.
Emphasize jumping up and not forward. (T)
2 Weight on hands — practise cartwheel.
□ Practise headstand, as in Unit 3, Lesson 2 (p. 75).
□ Partner sequence — balance → roll → weight on hands → balance.
It would be useful to write this sequence on a (T) blackboard or on a card for the children to read themselves.

LESSON 4

Equipment

Springboard, vaulting horse, balance beam, one beanbag and ball, a small mat each.

Warm-up

'Find a partner' — two to three children are 'he', the others are safe when with a partner. You may only stay with a partner for the count of three.

Skills

□ Balance on any number of body supports, with the body stretched.
□ Balance on any number of body supports, with the body twisted.

Application

Groups rotate between the following activities.
1 With teacher supervision, practise jumping on (one foot take-off) springboard and off (two foot take-off).
□ Introduce side vault with vaulting horse at lower level.

(T) Place hands on horse from side. Jump up and lift hips up high, tuck knees close to stomach and land with feet on horse. When children are confident with this and getting their hips high enough they can try to lift their legs right over.

2 Experiment with different ways of walking across beam — forwards, sideways, backwards, heel to toe, balancing beanbag on head, bouncing a ball.

LESSON 5

Equipment
Springboard, vaulting horse, balance beam, large mats, two hoops and two balls.

Warm-up
'Birds in the trees' — children in groups of three except for three to four spare birds. The two outside players of each three make trees by joining hands. At a signal, all birds change houses and spare birds try to find a home too.

Skills
☐ In groups of three — two children stand arms distance apart, while the third runs up, places his/her hands on the shoulders, lifts legs up high and jumps through. Swap over positions.

(T) Emphasize lifting hips high.

Application
Groups rotate between following activities.
1 Lead up to through vault using springboard and horse (with teacher supervision).
Two children sit on horse with arms supporting weight on arms. Other children run up, jump, place hands on shoulders and bring feet to land on horse.
☐ Repeat above, but go right through (teacher supports from the front).

2 In pairs, work out the following sequence on mats and take it in turns to practise on beam. Different way to centre of beam → stationary balance → different way to get off beam. (Hoops and balls can be used if children wish.)

LESSON 6

Equipment
Horse, springboard, large mats, two long ropes, balance beam, trampet, twelve hoops, ten balls.

Warm-up
Find a partner — as in Unit 3 Lesson 4 (p. 76). Leapfrog — groups of four make a line and leapfrog to line and back one after the other.

Skills/Application
☐ Gymnastics circuit — children rotate around equipment, starting at different points.
Regularly stop circuit to demonstrate the (T) different movements children are to do.
Try to get children to do something different from the person in front.
Hoops and balls are placed at various activities.
Teacher supervises the trampet.

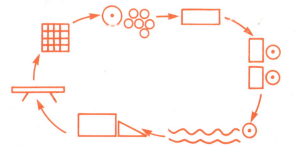

GRADES 3~4
Ball Handling

The children will experience hitting, bouncing, rolling, stopping, using bats, hockey sticks and cricket bats.

Helpful hints

☐ When two pieces of equipment need to be handed out, have the equipment in two different areas.

☐ If children are working with partners, one child can collect the ball and one can collect the bat.

☐ Letting children pick teams always leaves the less skilled child last to be picked, which is not very good for the self-image.

☐ Having a demonstration prepared keeps the lesson flowing.

☐ Use different children to give demonstrations.

☐ The less skilled child can be partnered with a more proficient child without too much fuss.

☐ Reward and encourage triers.

☐ Are the children keen to demonstrate their skills?

LESSON 1

Equipment
A tennis ball each, a bat each (rounders, bat-tennis) one hoop between two.

Warm-up
'Jockeys and wild horses' — four jockeys are selected and given a stable in the four corners of the area. Other players gallop around. On 'go' the jockeys catch as many horses as possible, leading one to the stable before catching the next. When caught, the horses cannot break away. When all horses are caught, the jockey with the most horses wins.

Skills
- Move the ball with the bat in as many different ways as possible, e.g. hit, bounce, roll.
- Keep the ball on the ground.
- Keep the ball in the air.
- ⒟ Alternate between keeping the ball in the air and on the ground.
- Hit the ball along the ground away from you. Run after it and stop it with your bat.
- In pairs, roll ball so your partner stops it with the bat.
- Roll ball so your partner has to move to stop the ball.
- Bounce the ball to each other, using bats.

Application
- Mini-tennis — children in pairs with one ball make up their own game and scoring system. They may use a hoop if they wish.
- Partners race against each other: partner A bounces ball up to line and back and partner B can follow on.
- Roll ball up to line and back.
- Balance ball up to line and back.

LESSON 2

Equipment
One bat and ball between two, one hoop between two.

Warm-up
'Train chasey' — children in pairs with one player left. Each pair forms a train, the front the engine and the back the carriage. The odd player tries to attach himself/herself to the back of one of the trains. When this has been achieved, the engine of that train has to drop off and attach himself/herself to another train.

Skills
- In pairs, with one bat and ball between two, one child passes ball to partner in any way so that he/she can hit it back, e.g. bounce and hit, roll and hit, throw and hit, throw low and hit, throw high and hit. Swap over bat to partner.

- Swap hands when hitting ball (right and left).
- Children join inner hands and alternately hit ball — try it walking!
- Partner A bounces ball to B who tries to hit ball into a hoop.

Application
- Hitting against team running — children are divided into two teams. Each player in team A runs around the netball court (or similar distance). Team B stand in a circle with a bat each and one person in the centre, who hits the ball to each person in the circle, counting the number of hits they get in the time it takes all of Team A to complete their run. Teams swap over and see who gets the most number of hits.

LESSON 3

Equipment
One bat and ball each, five hoops.

Warm-up

'Group chase' — one person is 'he' and tags others who join on hands thus making groups of two, three and four. Groups of four then divide into two couples who continue to chase, tag and divide until there is only one person left.

Skills

- Hit the ball in the air as many times as you can.
- Try various patterns, e.g. bounce once, hit in air once, bounce twice, hit in air twice, bounce three times, hit in air for three, and so on.

Application

- Bowler rounders — two teams, one batting, one fielding, played on a rounders diamond or similar marked by hoops. Bowler bounces ball to batter. When the ball is hit the batter attempts to run to first base before the fielders return the ball to the bowler. Any base runners between the bases when the bowler has the ball, are out. A batter can also be caught out. If three are out, side is out. A runner may pass another. There may be more than one runner at the base. Wait until the batter has a hit — don't count the strikes. The teacher can bowl for both teams.

LESSON 4

Equipment

A hockey stick each, one tennis ball between two, a block each.

Warm-up

'Jockeys and wildhorses' — as in Unit 3, Lesson 1 (p. 79).

Skills

- Hit the ball along the ground to each other using the hockey sticks.
- Try and hit through two blocks to partner.

Gradually decrease the distance between the blocks as the skill increases and also increase the distance from the blocks.

Application

- Corner relay — children in groups of six to eight. Number six hits the ball to number one and so on to number five, who runs out and takes number six's position and continues the pattern. Number six goes to number one's position and everyone else moves up one place.

- Hitting against team running — as in Unit 3, Lesson 2 (p. 79), except hockey sticks are used and the ball is hit on the ground.

LESSON 5

Equipment

A cricket bat between two (or rounders bat), a tennis ball between two, one hoop between two, two blocks.

Warm-up

'Train chasey' — as in Unit 3, Lesson 2 (p. 79).

Skills

- Children hit the ball to each other using a cricket bat — one bowls ball and the other hits back.
- Partner hits back so bowler can catch the ball — see how many hits and catches you can get in a row.
- Partner hits back to try and get the ball to bounce in a hoop.

Application

- Circle cricket — in groups of four or five, one person bats while the others field the ball and attempt to hit the batter with the ball below the knees. If hit, or if caught on the full, batter is out and next person bats.
- Hit the block — two groups of twelve to fourteen. The players around the circle aim the ball at the block in the centre of the circle that the batter protects with his bat. Once the block is hit the thrower has a hit.

with a partner and one at a time stand near the batter and run when the ball is hit. The fielders can catch the runners out, or field the ball and throw it to a base to which the couple are running. The couple are out if they don't reach the base before the fielder has the ball and a foot in the base. When three runners are out, the team changes over. No more than one couple on one base at a time.

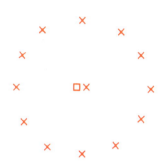

LESSON 6

Equipment

Five hoops (or rounders diamond), one rounders bat, one tennis ball.

Warm-up

'Group chase' — as in Unit 3, Lesson 3 (p. 80).

Skills/Application

- Partner rounders — class is divided into two equal teams. One batter has five hits in a row and doesn't run or go out (runners are out instead). The other members of the team are

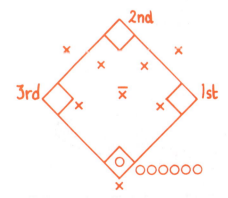

GRADES 3~4
Athletics

The children will experience discus, triple jump, revision of previous units.

Helpful hints

- Emphasize the safety aspect when using equipment. Keep the lesson closely monitored when using equipment such as the discus.
- Make sure all children are watching any demonstrations.
- Use questioning techniques to make sure that the correct technique has been understood.
- Allow sufficient time for practising the skills.
- This unit allows scope to develop the concept of children coaching each other.
- Make it known if an individual has improved.
- Is everyone enjoying P. E.?

LESSON 1

Equipment
One cane each, skipping ropes.

Warm-up
'Find a partner' — choose three to four children to be 'he', who chase the others. A player is not out if standing with a partner. You can only stand with another person until the count of three. Stretching — make large and small circles with your arms; bend sideways with legs astride; walk hands forward, while feet are still and legs straight, then walk feet to hands.

Skills
- Triple jump (hop, step and jump).
- Practise long jumping.
- Run around and see how far you can jump.
- Try the following:
  a The hop — take off and land on the same foot.
  b The step — take off from one foot and land on the other.
  c The jump — take off from one foot and land on both feet.
- Divide the class into three groups, each group has three cane sticks set out like a ladder. Hop over the first, step over the second and jump over the third. Start from a standing position, or running approaches with canes further apart as required.

(T) Discuss the type of run-up that will give you the best jump.

Application
- Jumping the creek — make two lines with ropes/canes for banks of the creek, gradually increasing the width. Children triple jump the creek (with the last jump). Those who successfully jump all sections begin at the narrow end with standing triple jumps to see how far they can get.

LESSON 2

Equipment
Ten small gym mats, ten blocks, five canes.

Warm-up
'Jail tiggy' — one person is the guard, another the chaser, the other children spread out in restricted area. An area is made for a jail (approx. 3 metres square) where tagged children go until released. This release can be made by a free player tagging anyone in the jail. The guard attempts to tag anyone who comes close to the jail. Meanwhile the chaser attempts to tag as many players as possible. Change guard and chaser regularly.
Stretching — leg stretches to both sides; sideways bend to both sides; knee roll — tuck knees into chest and rock sideways.

Skills
- Triple jump — revise skills learnt in Lesson 1.
- Revise skills of long jump.

Application
- Hop, step and jump the creek — approx. ten small gym mats are set out like stepping stones in a creek. The aim is to get from numbers one to ten without touching the ground. This can be done by stepping, hopping or jumping, as decided by the teacher. Increase the distances as children have completed the course. Add obstacles such as canes on blocks to make it more difficult.

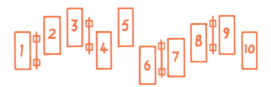

LESSON 3

Equipment
Discus — as many as possible, or anything similar, e.g. rubber rings. Eight blocks.

Warm-up
'Here, there, nowhere' — when teacher says 'here', run in direction indicated by teacher. The teacher then quickly changes to 'there' and points in a different direction. On 'nowhere', run on spot.
Stretching — legs astride, knees bent, alternately touch hands to opposite toes; arm circles — as in Unit 3, Lesson 1; leg stretches to each side.

Skills
Holding the discus — with palm facing down, arm out to side; place the fingers over discus to (T) (D)

the top joint; lay the thumb flat against the discus; swing the arm backwards and forth. The discus should stay in the hand.
Rolling the discus — hold the discus vertical and roll it along the ground.

Application
☐ Roll a goal — four teams line up and using the above method, see how many goals they can roll.

LESSON 4

Equipment
Discus/rubber rings, four blocks.

Warm-up
'Object relay' — five teams in relay formation. The first runner from each team runs to touch four points as stated by teacher, e.g. netball post, wall, door, fence, etc. and then returns to their team to tag the next runner. When tagged the second runner completes the same course and so on.
Stretching — choose four different children to lead the class in a stretch for a specific area.

Skills
(T) Teaching points for throwing the discus. Turn sideways so the opposite foot to the throwing arm is at the front of the circle and the toe of this foot is on a straight line with the heel of the right foot. Swing forward and back as in previous lesson and then release the discus in a standing throw. Try and make the discus fly flat.
☐ Practise throwing the discus.
(T) Keep the children in lines (relay formation), they throw when teacher indicates, and collect discus when teacher indicates.

Application
☐ Hit the block — children in relay formation, one at a time throw the discus to see if they can hit the block.

LESSON 5

Equipment
One ball, four batons, shots.

Warm-up
Run around the school block or similar area. Stretching — four different children each take a stretch each.

Skills
☐ Revise technique for triple jump as in Unit 3, Lesson 1 (p. 83).
☐ Revise sprinting technique, including the crouch start.
☐ Revise throwing of the shot.

Children stand in relay formation. Monitor the (T) throwing and collecting.

Application
☐ Sprinting against catches in a circle — divide class into two teams, one person at a time from team A sprints a determined distance, while team B see how many catches they can get in a circle in the same time. Teams swap over activities to see who can get the most catches.
☐ Shuttle relay — children in relay formation, pass the baton to next person in their team.

LESSON 6

Equipment
Discus, shot.

Skills/Application
The following events could be performed on athletics day. Divide class into four teams.
☐ Everybody runs around school boundary/ oval once.
☐ Discus, shot-put, long jump, triple jump activities spread around oval. Teams rotate around activities, spending approximately four minutes at each activity. Children aim to beat a standard set down, e.g. throw discus over a line a set distance out; put shot over a line a set distance out; long jump over a line a set distance out; triple jump over a line a set distance out. Children can score a point each time they beat the standard.
☐ Shuttle relay.

GRADES 3~4
Minor Games/Fitness

The children will experience partner activities, relays, group games, skipping, hopscotch.

Helpful hints
- Use different children and teams to demonstrate activities.
- Have demonstrations ready in advance with the children involved.
- Try and make sure the children are active and energetic.
- Try to develop good team involvement.
- Have competitions, but make sure children are enjoying the games and the competition isn't taking over.
- Give positive reinforcement to straight, quiet lines.

LESSON 1

Equipment
One ball between two.

Warm-up
'Fight the bombers!' — as in Unit 1, Lesson 3 — Minor games (p. 59).

Skills
PARTNER ACTIVITIES
- In pairs, one ball between two, partners stand back to back, bend and pass the ball through legs and then over head. See how many passes you can get in a minute.
- Side to side passing — standing back to back pass the ball sideways to each other as many times as possible in a minute.

- Circle the bouncing ball — partner A bounces ball as high as he/she can, while partner B runs around the ball as many times as he/she can. Partner A rolls ball to line, while partner B chases and picks up after reaching line.
- Partner relays — each team consists of pairs who run to line and back. The teacher gives a variety of activities, e.g. holding hands, running back to back, bottoms touching.
- Tunnel ball relay — first person rolls ball through tunnel. Last person gathers ball and runs up to line, followed by rest of team and back to line up. He/she then rolls the ball.
- Through the legs relay — legs astride, end players start by crawling through the legs, then second last players and so on, until the first person ends up in the front.

GAMES
- Dodge the ball — as in Unit 2, Lesson 1 — Minor games (p. 72).

LESSON 2

Equipment
Four canes, one ball.

Warm-up
'Hunters and hares' — as in Unit 2, Lesson 5 — Minor games (p. 73).

Skills
PARTNER ACTIVITIES
- Partner run — partner A stands on one side of centre line and B on the other. On 'go', A runs to respective sideline and returns to touch B's hand, B then runs to line and back to A. See how many times partners can touch hands in one minute. Variation: hop, skip.
- Wheelbarrows.
- Touch hands — children stand back to back, bend over and touch hands between their legs, then stretch up to touch hands above their head.
- Hop and pull — partners face each other, grasp left hands and their own raised left ankle with right hands. Each tries to pull their partner off balance with hopping and pulling movements.

RELAYS
- Jump the stick — as in Unit 1, Lesson 1 — Minor games/fitness (p. 59).
- Partner relays — as in Unit 3, Lesson 1.

- Square run — number one runs around square to tag number two who runs around and tags number three and so on. Repeat two to three times.

- Through the legs relay — as in Unit 3, Lesson 1.

GAMES
- Hit the tail. Circle formation, five children in centre holding each other's waists. Outside players throw ball to hit the last person. The leader of the tail is the only one allowed to hit the ball with hands or feet. As the tail is hit, the player joins the circle until only one is left. The leader can also go out if he/she hits the ball back to the circle and is caught on the full.

LESSON 3

Equipment
One long skipping rope, one hoop each.

Warm-up
Run around school block, oval etc. once or twice.

Skills/Application
Hoops (one hoop each).
- Skip with hoop.
- Spin hoop forward to make it come back.
- Spin hoop around waist, leg, arm, neck.
- Hoop on ground — jump in and out, hop in and out, jump in, hop out.
- Crawl through hoop, run to line and back.

Let children make up various movements with the hoop.

(T)

SKIPPING
- Revise Unit 2 activities (p. 73), i.e. individuals running though — miss loops, miss no loops, with jumps, with partners. Various rhymes can be introduced — many of which the children will know or they can be found in books.

LESSON 4

Equipment
A skipping rope, counters (hopscotch), hopscotch markings.

Warm-up
'Fight the bombers.'

Skills
HOPSCOTCH
- Introduce 'normal' hopscotch rules, set up several games with 4–5 per group.
- Games can be chalked onto asphalt, taped on, but preferably painted on.

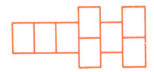

SKIPPING
- As in Unit 3, Lesson 3.

GAMES
- Cars — players, in relay formation, are given names of cars coinciding in each line. When teacher calls out a car name the player from each team runs to line and back. On 'all cars', all players, one at a time starting from back crawl through legs of those in front, run to line and back. First team with straight line wins a point.

LESSON 5

Equipment
One ball, counters (hopscotch), hopscotch markings.

Warm-up
'Hunters and hares' (see p. 73).

Skills
HOPSCOTCH
- Introduce other variations:

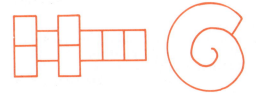

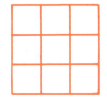

Square hopscotch — both feet in middle square of first row; one foot in two outside squares of first row; both feet in middle square of first row; hop out. Repeat above in second then third row. Repeat above, doing it backwards.
Snail hopscotch — variations: hop all the way around without touching a line. Throw counter into first square, hop in and pick up marker and hop backwards out. Throw counter into second square, hop into first pick up counter and hop backwards out and so on. Normal hopscotch — as in Unit 3, Lesson 4.

GAME
- Dodge the ball.

LESSON 6

Equipment
Counters (hopscotch), long skipping rope, one ball.

Warm-up
'Continuous tiggy' — four players are 'he'. They try to tag as many players as possible. When caught, the player joins hands and so on until no-one is left.

Skills
PARTNER ACTIVITIES
- Partner run as in Unit 3, Lesson 2 (p. 86).
- Wheelbarrows.
- Hop and pull — as in Unit 3, Lesson 2 (p. 86).

HOPSCOTCH
- As in Unit 3, Lessons 4 and 5.

SKIPPING
- As in Unit 3, Lesson 3.

Children in small groups could rotate around the various hopscotch activities and the skipping (with teacher supervision).

GAMES
- Dodge ball.
- Cars — as in Unit 3, Lesson 4.
- Hit the tail — as in Unit 3, Lesson 2 (p. 86).

GRADES 5~6
Gymnastics

The children will experience running, balance, rolling, jumping, rocking, weight on hands, sequence development.

Helpful hints

- Emphasize the need for children to sit properly while listening to you. An easy form is 'long sit' where children sit with legs straight out and hands by side.
- Instead of using the whistle for gymnastics you can use 'and long sit'. Children respond very well to this, especially with some positive reinforcement.
- Gymnastics activities always require children to be sensible and to concentrate as accidents can easily happen.
- Take advantage of any child's creativity, gymnastics gives them an excellent opportunity to create new ideas.
- The less skilled child can be partnered with a more proficient child without too much fuss.

RELATED CLASSROOM ACTIVITIES

Minor theme — our body

Children should be aware of the major systems and functions of the body.

- Skeletal — the structure of the body.
- Muscular — how the body moves.
- Respiratory — how the body breathes.
- Circulatory — the movement of blood and nutrients.
- Digestive — what provides the energy.

Minor theme — nutrition

- Why do we need food in our body?
- What food do we need for a healthy body?
- Charts could be made of the five main food groups.
- Differences can be shown between processed and unprocessed food. Children can make a list of the processed and unprocessed food in their home.

Minor theme — leisure, games and fitness

- Children analyse how active they are. A timetable can be made for them to fill in the different types of activities they do at school. Distinction should be made between the different activities, whether they cause the heart to work very hard, or whether they require little effort.
- Children change a habit to make them more active.
- Children are asked to record the amount of sleep they have a week and if it's sufficient. Discuss why regular sleep is important.
- Children investigate various games they are interested in — rules, etiquette etc. Models could be made of various games.

LESSON 1

Equipment
A small mat each.

Warm-up
Run forwards then change to hopping forwards.
Run and hop, but change direction on signal.
Jump up and land deeply from a crouch position.
(T) Land with bent knees.
Jump up making different shapes in the air —
wide, thin, twisted.

Skills
(D) □ **Balance** on various body supports, e.g. on
one foot and two hands, on two feet and one
hand, on three, four or five body supports.
□ Introduce 'V' balance — raise feet up in front
of face while sitting down, arms extended
behind body.

□ With body support of shoulders and bottom,
rock in a wide shape.
□ Rock in a curled shape, any body supports.
□ Rock in a wide shape, any body supports.
□ Curled **roll** in any direction.
□ Thin roll in sideways direction.
□ Weight on hands — move on two hands and
two feet, facing up, facing down, change
direction.

Application
□ In pairs, develop a sequence of: wide
balance → curled shape → wide balance.
(T) Encourage a smooth sequence.
(D) Give demonstrations of different ideas.

LESSON 2

Equipment
A small mat per child, a hoop each.

Warm-up
Run around area alternating between stretching

high and bending low.
Run with changes of speed and direction, e.g.
backwards and slow, upwards and moderate,
sideways and fast.
Jump in and out of hoop in various shapes.
Touch various parts of body while jumping in
and out.

Skills
□ Balancing — make a bridge balance over
hoop.
□ Balance inside the hoop on three body
supports with head as the highest part.
□ Rolling — revise teaching points for a
forward roll.
Hands shoulder-width apart, head tucked in, (T)
look through legs, hands used to push up.
□ Forward roll with variations — different
starting positions, e.g. squatting, kneeling,
walking.
□ Forward roll through hoop (held by partner).
□ Weight on hands — free practice to explore
leg shapes in air — wide, curled.
□ Introduce frogstand:

Kneel on knees, sit back on heels, place your (D)
hands so that fingers are in line with knees.
Place head on mat. Raise hips high and
straighten knees. Place knees one at a time on
elbows. Children practise with partner
supporting backs.

Application
□ Change places with each other by: a jump (D)
low to the ground; a thin roll; a different type
of jump.

LESSON 3

Equipment
A cane between two, small mat each.

Warm-up
In pairs, jump over cane in various ways,
gradually increasing height.

89

Skills
- ☐ Roll slowly over cane held by partner.
- ☐ Roll quickly under cane held by partner.
- ☐ Introduce 'dive roll'.

Ⓣ Reach further out than for a forward roll, keep head between arms and tucked, strong drive through legs initially, weight on hands when landing.
- ☐ Weight on hands — find various ways in which the feet land in a different place from that of take-off.
- ☐ Revise frogstand as in Unit 1, Lesson 2 (p. 89).
- ☐ Partner A kneels, partner B must balance part of his/her body on A and part on the floor.
- ☐ Partner A has three body supports, partner B two body supports.

Application
Ⓓ ☐ Partner sequence — jump over cane in any shape → own choice of balance → any slow roll to change places with partner. Partner then repeats using different shapes.

LESSON 4

Equipment
A small mat each.

Warm-up
Run and jump making wide shapes in the air. Try to touch your feet while jumping.

Skills
- ☐ Jumping — introduce 'flea hop'

Kneeling on mat with arms behind hips while leaning forward slightly. Vigorously throw arms forward and upward to jump up from the knees to land on feet. Ⓣ
- ☐ In pairs try balances where one partner has no body parts on the ground.

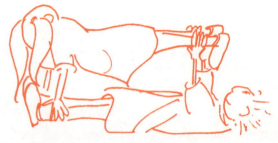

☐ Introduce backward straddle roll.
Starting position — legs straight and apart, sit backwards with hands by ears, push with feet and hands, keep legs straight. Ⓣ
- ☐ Practise backward straddle roll with a partner.
- ☐ Revise dive roll, over partner.
- ☐ Weight on hands — revise frogstand.

Application
- ☐ Partner sequence — any slow roll to change Ⓓ places with partner → any wide jump to change places with partner → any quick roll to change places with partner → partner balance.

LESSON 5

Equipment
A small gym mat each.

Warm-up
'Follow the leader' in groups of four to five, slow changes in direction, speed and length of stride. Regularly change leaders by the leader going to Ⓣ the back of the line.

Skills
- ☐ Jumping — revise 'flea hop', as in Unit 1, Lesson 4.
- ☐ 'Echo balance' — partner copies balance Ⓓ demonstrated by partner.
- ☐ Revise balances where whole of body weight is supported by partner (as in Unit 1, Lesson 4).
- ☐ Introduce backward roll.

(T) Squat and sit on heels. Rock back vigorously and pull hips over head. Practise this a few times. Place hands behind shoulders, as hips come over, push up with hands. Keep knees and feet tucked. Partners help each other by supporting back from the side view.

(D) □ Try a one-handed forward roll.

(D) □ Forward roll from kneeling position with arms folded.

(D) □ Forward roll as above from standing position.

Application

(D) □ Partner sequence — jump → roll → balance.

LESSON 6

Equipment
A small mat each, cane between two.

Warm-up
In pairs — standing jump over cane, gradually increasing height.
Running jump over cane, gradually increasing height.
Scissors jump over cane, gradually increasing height.

Skills
□ Balance in groups of four with the following limitations:
    one person has no body supports
    one person has four body supports
    two people have two body supports.
Variations: all have two body supports; other variations can be included.
□ Revise backward roll.
□ Revise backward straddle roll.
□ Try any wide roll/curled roll in different direction.
□ In pairs, try a forward roll from a wheelbarrow walk.

Application
□ Sequence with group of four: weight on hands activity → roll — any direction or shape → balance.

(T) Encourage cooperation with group members.

(D) Give various demonstrations
Look for quality of movement and a smooth sequence.

GRADES 5~6
Ball Handling

The children will experience rolling, catching, stopping, throwing.

Helpful hints

- Monitors can be responsible for collecting and handing out equipment.
- Children with discipline problems can be given responsibility by helping to hand out equipment with a more responsible child.
- On whistle, 'stop' and place ball between feet on ground.
- When giving demonstrations, all children should be listening and watching with ball between their feet.
- Use different people to give demonstrations.
- Are the children keen to demonstrate their skills?

LESSON 1

Equipment
A ball each, a block each (or chalk).

Warm-up
'Jockeys and wild horses' — four jockeys are selected and given a stable in the four corners of the area. Other players gallop around. On 'go' the jockeys catch as many horses as possible, leading one to the stable before catching the next. When caught the horses cannot break away. When all horses are caught, the jockey with the most horses wins.

Skills
- Roll the ball using various body parts.
- Roll the ball along a line, run and stop it with your feet.
- Roll the ball so it stops as close as possible to a line.
- (T) Release ball close to the ground so it does not bounce.
  Opposite foot forward to rolling arm.
  Follow through with hand in direction of roll.
- Roll ball to a partner using both hands, right/left hands.
- Roll ball through partner's legs — gradually increase distance.

Application
- Rolling for accuracy — children in pairs attempt to roll the ball between the two blocks (or marks with chalk)
- Increase distance of roll and bring blocks closer together to increase difficulty.

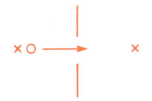

LESSON 2

Equipment
One ball between two, one block between two.

Warm-up
'Find a partner' — choose four children to be 'he' who chase the others. A player is not out if standing with a partner. You can only stand with another person for the count of three.

Skills
- In pairs, roll ball to a line, between two lines; to hit a block; between two blocks.
- Partner A rolls ball from leg to leg (whilst standing legs astride) while the other partner runs around him/her three times. Swap over and see who can do it the most number of times.

Application
Relays in groups of eight:
- 'A' rolls ball through blocks to 'B' who continues on and 'A' runs to end of opposite line.

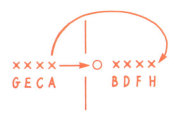

- Tunnel ball — roll ball through legs and run to front. Variation: roll ball to front of line rather than running.
- Circle ball — players in circle formation in astride position pass the ball along the ground anywhere in the circles trying to pass the ball between a player's legs. This player defends by using hands only. Variation: use two balls.

LESSON 3

Equipment
One ball between two.

Warm-up
'Train chasey' — children in pairs with one player left. Each pair forms a train, the front the engine and the back the carriage. The odd player tries to attach himself/herself to the back of one of the trains. If successful, the engine of that train has to drop off and attach himself/herself to another train.

Skills
- Stop a ball — rolled straight to the body; rolled to the side of the body; bouncing along the ground; thrown at different heights, e.g. above head, near the ground; travelling in the same direction as the person is running;

rolled at various speeds.

(T) Move into the line of the ball, watching it all the time.
Allow the ball to come into your hands.
Point fingers to the ground.
Bend back and legs.

Application
- 'Beat the middle' — six to eight players pass the ball across a circle, no higher than half a metre above the head. A player in the centre tries to stop the ball, if successful he/she exchanges places with the player who threw the ball. If, after ten throws, the ball has not been caught, the player with the ball becomes the new person in the centre.
- Circle ball — as in Unit 1, Lesson 2 (p. 93).

LESSON 4

Equipment
A ball each.

Warm-up
'Jockeys and wild horses' — as in Unit 1, Lesson 1 (p. 93).

Skills
- Catching — throw in air, clap and catch. Throw in air, clap as many times as possible and catch. Throw in air, bounce, turn around and catch. Catch ball rebounding off a wall. Catch on full. Touch ground and catch. Turn around and catch.
- In pairs, catch ball rebounding off wall thrown by partner. Catch ball bounced by partner. Catch ball kicked by partner.

Application
- Name ball — in groups of eight, one ball each group. One player throws ball in air and calls the name of a player in the circle. If player catches it he/she throws it up and calls another name. If dropped, the player has to run after it and call 'stop' when he/she has it. He/she then throws it to try to hit someone, who, if hit becomes the next person to throw the ball and call someone's name.
- Ball chase — in groups of eight two balls per group. Two balls start on opposite sides of the circle and each ball tries to catch up to the other.

LESSON 5

Equipment
A ball each, chalk, two cricket stumps.

Warm-up
'Find a partner' as in Unit 1, Lesson 2 (p. 93).

Skills
- Throwing at wall — with two hands, with right/left hands, overarm, underarm.

Hold the ball with fingers and not the palm. (T)
Step with opposite foot to throwing hand in direction of throw.
Follow through with hand in direction of throw.
Elbow leads arm action and is followed by a straight arm
Throw at a target on wall, drawn with chalk (see diagrams), with both left and right hand.

Application
- Target ball — two even groups, two balls and one cricket stump per group. The players form a circle around the cricket stump. This is protected by a player who uses hands or feet to deflect or stop the balls. Any player who hits the stump changes places with the defender.
- Hit the tail — the whole class forms a circle with five children in centre holding waists. Outside players throw ball to hit the last person. The leader of the tail is the only one allowed to hit the ball with hands or feet. As the tail is hit, the player joins the circle, until only one is left. The leader of the tail can also get out if he/she hits the ball back on the full to the circle.

LESSON 6

Equipment
One ball between two, one block between two.

Warm-up
'Train chasey' — as in Unit 1, Lesson 3 (p. 93).

Skills

□ In pairs, facing each other, stand close together. Every time the ball is caught take a step out, when the ball is dropped, take a step in.

□ Throw to hit a block, increasing distance of throw as skill improves.

Application

□ Sprinting against catches in a circle — divide class into two teams, team A sprints a set distance one at a time, while team B sees how many catches they can get in a circle in the time it takes team A to complete their run. Teams swap over to see who gets the most catches.

□ Divide class into two even teams, with three to four balls. Team A aims to field the ball and hit the player from team A running up to line and back below the waist. If player reaches line and back without getting hit he/she scores a point. Roles reverse when all of team B have had a run.

□ Hit the tail — as in Unit 1, Lesson 5 (p. 94).

GRADES 5~6
Major Games

The children will experience the following skills of softball: overarm throw, underarm throw, fielding, baserunning, batting.

Helpful hints

- A lot of equipment is necessary, so have it ready before the lesson.
- Encourage the children to look after the equipment.
- Many demonstrations will be required to display various skills. Make sure all children are watching and the correct skill is displayed.
- Give the less skilled child individual goals to aim for.
- Try and encourage the children to coach each other.

LESSON 1

Equipment

One softball between two (tennis balls will suffice), as many gloves as possible.

Warm-up

'Group chase' — one player is 'he' and tags others who join on hands thus making groups of two, three and four. Groups of four then divide into two couples. The couples continue to chase, tag and divide until there is only one person left.

Skills

- ☐ Practise overarm throw to reach your partner at chest height.
- (T) Step forward with opposite foot to throwing arm. Lead throw with elbow, then straight out arm. Point arm in direction of throw.
- (D) ☐ Practise underarm throw. The ball should reach partner on the full at waist level.
- ☐ Catching with gloves, above the waist
- (T) Fingers of the gloved hand point upwards. The palm of the glove faces the ball. The glove receives the full force of the ball and the other hand quickly covers ball to stop it from bouncing out.
- (T) ☐ Catching with gloves below the waist. As above, except fingers point to the side rather than up. Partners throw ball high and low to practise catching.

Application

- ☐ In groups of six, leader A throws overarm to B who returns and bobs down. A then throws to C who returns and bobs down and so on.

```
    x        x x x x x
    A        B C D E F
```

- ☐ Leader underarms ball past line. Runs to stop it and throws ball back to next player. Each player has a turn.

```
    x x x x x x        | |
```

LESSON 2

Equipment

Softball diamond (or area marked by hoop), gloves, balls.

Warm-up

Base running — four even teams. Number one from each team circles the bases. He/she tags number two and lines up at the rear of the team. Run in a circular motion as shown. Run and touch bases on the inside. (T)

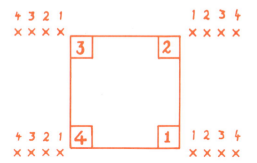

Skills

- ☐ Fielding ground ball — partner A throws a ground ball for B to field and throw back.
  Position body in line with ball, one foot in front of (T) the other, bending knees so the body is low to the ground. Watch ball all the time. Fingers pointing down and palms facing ball. Allow the hands to 'give' when the ball hits.

Application

- ☐ Divide the class into two even teams. The first member of each team rolls balls along the ground towards the opposite team, in an attempt to pass their line. If successful a point is scored.
- ☐ Base running against throwing — the ball is thrown from number one to number two around the diamond and back to number two. Meanwhile number one from the running team runs around the outside of the diamond and tries to beat the ball home. If successful, he/she scores a point. When all players have run, swap over.

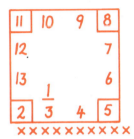

You might need to hold the runner back until the (T) ball has reached number five, depending on the skill level.

LESSON 3

Equipment
Softball bats, softballs, gloves, T ball stands.

Warm-up
Base running — as in Unit 1, Lesson 2 (p. 97).

Skills
- Batting.
- Grip — two-handed, 'shake hands' with bat, hands close together.
Stance — weight slightly more on back foot. Bat held comfortably back with upper arm parallel to ground.
Batting — keep bat parallel to ground when hitting; watch ball all the way; step forward with front foot as you bat; transfer body weight from back to front foot.
- Each child practises action with a bat. In two groups hit a stationary ball from T ball stand. Fielders retrieve ball and throw into catcher.

Application
- Divide class into four teams and have two games running concurrently. Team A fields the ball and gets it back to catcher as quickly as possible while team B, one at a time hits the ball, runs up to the line and back and if they beat the ball back score a point for their team. Swap over activities.

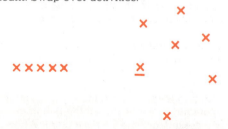

LESSON 4

Equipment
Balls, bats, gloves, T ball stands.

Warm-up
'Group chase' — as in Unit 1, Lesson 1 (p. 97).

Skills
- Batting — groups of six stand in the formation shown in the diagram. The player who fields the ball pitches it to the batter. Once batter has hit ball five times, change places. Batter should not attempt to hit the ball hard.

Application
- Hit the stand — four teams, with two games running concurrently. Batter hits ball into circle and aims to run around the circle before the fielders stop the ball and hit the stand. Fielders can only hit the stand from the outside of the circle. If the batter gets back before the stand is hit he/she scores a point for the team. If batters are getting around too easily, place four bases around circle and run around these instead.

LESSON 5

Equipment
Softball kit.

Warm-up
'Fight the bombers' — bombers formed by couples joining inner hands, move freely within area. Three to four players are fighters and attempt to shoot the bombers by tagging them. When tagged, the bombers must stand and make an archway with hands held up high. They can be freed to rejoin the game by another bomber flying through their archway. Change fighters regularly.

Skills/Application
- Run till you're out — played like regular softball with the sides changing at three out. The hitter must continue running the bases until he/she is out. If he/she is safe at first base he/she scores one point, two to reach second base, three for third and four for home. The first team to score twenty-five points is the winner, or the team with the

most number of points at the end of time is
the winner.

Equipment
Softball kit, four blocks.

Warm-up
Run around oval or school boundary.

Skills/Application
☐   Beat the blocks — divide the class into two
teams. The batter, after hitting the ball into
the diamond, circles the bases to home
before the fielders are able to knock down
the blocks with the ball. The fielders retrieve
ball and pass it to any base first, then around
to the remainder. As the baseman receives
the ball he/she knocks down the block and
throws to the next base. The batter is out if
caught by a fly ball. Scoring — if batter
completes the bases without a block being
knocked down, score two runs. If batter beats
ball home, score one run. If fielders can
knock down three of the blocks the batter
only scores half a run.

GRADES 5~6
Minor Games/Fitness

The children will experience partner activities, relays, group games, distance running.

Helpful hints

- Regularly revise boundaries to be used.
- The most important aspects of these sessions are for the children to be actively involved as much as possible and for them to display good team involvement.
- Have demonstrations prepared in advance so that the demonstration is correct for the rest of the class to see.
- Try to encourage children to play cooperatively in small groups.
- Keep children happy and healthy!

LESSON 1

Equipment
Four canes, four balls.

Warm-up
'Group chase' — one person is 'he' and tags others who join hands thus making groups of two, three or four. Groups of four then divide into two couples. The couples continue to chase, tag and divide until there is only one person left.

PARTNER ACTIVITIES
- Circle run — one partner stands with hand up in front of body. The other partner runs around him/her and hits the hand as he/she passes. After five times, partners change places.
- Touch hands — partners stand back to back, bend over and touch hands between their legs and then above their head.
- Through the legs — one partner stands feet astride and one hand out. The other partner runs behind and through the legs, stands and hits his/her partner's hand. Change places every five turns.
- Knee chasey — partner A is chased by B until B can touch A behind the knee. The roles are changed every 30 seconds. Stay within a small area.

RELAYS
- Run to line and back, tag the next person.
- Jump the stick — the first person runs with cane to touch the line and returns down the side of the team holding the stick low to the ground. As he/she passes, each team member jumps over the cane. Pass the cane on to number two.
- Carry your toes — the first person hops to the line holding his/her toes and sprints back.
- Trains — number one runs to line forwards and back backwards. He/she picks up the next person and takes him/her up to the line and runs backwards to pick up the next person and so on.

GAMES
- Tunnel ball.

LESSON 2

Equipment
Nil.

Warm-up
'Fight the bombers' — bombers formed by couples joining inner hands, move freely within the area. Three to four players are fighters and attempt to shoot the bombers by tagging them. When tagged, the bombers must stand and make an archway with hands held above heads. They can be freed to rejoin the game by another bomber flying through their archway. Change fighters regularly.

PARTNER ACTIVITIES
- Partner standing — partners sit back to back with knees bent and arms interlocked. Try and stand up together with backs remaining together. Sit and stand again.
- Hopping bumps — partners hold up one leg and place their other hand behind their back. They then bump each other until one places the other foot on the ground.
- Knee chasey — as in Unit 1, Lesson 1.
- Through the legs — as in Unit 1, Lesson 1.

GAMES
- Through the legs — Children in groups of three to four run freely within the area. On whistle, the leader of each team stands with legs wide while other team members run to crawl through leader's legs. As each member passes he/she stands up, legs wide, thereby extending tunnel for others to crawl through. The first team to line up scores a point. On whistle, leader crawls through legs followed by rest of the team until all are running.
- Dog and cat — double circle facing centre. One pair is selected, one being the dog and the other the cat. The dog chases the cat and the cat plays safe by standing behind a pair. This makes the front player into a cat and the game continues.
Encourage cats to change all the time. ⓣ
- Boats — groups of four players form a file with hands on hips of person in front. On a signal the team hops on right legs to line and then reverse order and direction to hop back to starting line on left legs.

LESSON 3

Equipment
Ten balls, twelve beanbags.

Warm-up
'Chase the beanbag' — twelve children hold a beanbag. A person is 'he' and tries to tag a

player with a beanbag. If successful a new chaser is chosen. Children should be encouraged to run and dodge, but if capture is close, throw the beanbag to another player.

PARTNER ACTIVITIES
- Partner run — partner A stands on one side of centre line and partner B on the other. On 'go', A runs to the line and returns to touch B's hand. B then runs to line and back to A. See how many times partners touch hands in one minute.
- Hand jump — partner A holds hand high. From a standing position B jumps up to touch A's hand with his/her hand. If successful, repeat from a crouch position.
- Partner standing — as in Unit 1, Lesson 2 (p. 101).
- Hopping bumps — as in Unit 1, Lesson 2 (p. 101).

RUNNING
- Children run around school boundary with the following variations: Walk fifty steps, run fifty steps around the school boundary. Run to first corner, throw and catch ball ten times, run to second corner, touch toes ten times, run to third corner — bounce and catch ball ten times, run to fourth corner — do ten sit ups. Children set off at different time intervals and perform as many activities as they can.

GAME
- Poison ball — use two balls.

LESSON 4

Equipment
Four canes, eight hoops, eight blocks.

Warm-up
'Group chase' — as in Unit 1, Lesson 1 (p. 101).

PARTNER ACTIVITIES
- Partner cars — partners face each other with hands on shoulders. Partner A moves backwards while B steers. On signal reverse order.
- Side to side — partners stand back to back. With arms sideways they clasp hands and bend from side to side to touch knees.
- Partner run — as in Unit 1, Lesson 3.
- Hand jump — as in Unit 1, Lesson 3.

RELAYS
- Jump the stick — as in Unit 1, Lesson 1 (p. 101).
- Trains — as in Unit 1, Lesson 1 (p. 101).
- Jump the river — number one runs behind his/her team who are sitting on ground with legs out straight and jumps over legs and back to his/her place. Number two continues and so on.
- Knock the blocks — two hoops are placed on ground with two blocks inside A. Number one runs to A, pushes over the blocks with his/her elbow and then takes the blocks, one at a time to hoop B. Number one returns and number two goes to B and repeats the sequence.

GAMES
- Dog and cat — as in Unit 1, Lesson 2 (p. 101).
- Through the legs — as in Unit 1, Lesson 2 (p. 101).

LESSON 5

Equipment
One ball.

Warm-up
'Fight the bombers' — as in Unit 1, Lesson 2 (p. 101).

PARTNER ACTIVITIES
- Sideways slipping — partners stand back to back, arms interlocked. From the line they move sideways with side slipping to the line and back. Repeat several times.
- Partner cars — as in Unit 1, Lesson 4.
- Side to side — as in Unit 1, Lesson 4.
- Hopping wrestle — partners stand on one foot and hold opponent's hand. With hopping and pulling movements each partner tries to unbalance the other.

RUNNING
- Children divide into groups of eight and

follow the leader around the school
boundary/oval. Swap leaders after fifty steps.

GAMES
- Hit the tail — the whole class forms a circle
  with five children in centre holding waists.
  Outside players throw ball to hit the last
  person. The leader of the tail is the only one
  allowed to hit the ball with hands or feet. As
  the tail is hit, the player joins the circle, until
  only one is left. The leader of the tail can also
  go out if he/she hits the ball back to the
  circle and is caught on the full.

LESSON 6

Equipment
Two balls.

Warm-up
'Through the legs' — as in Unit 1, Lesson 2
(p. 101).

PARTNER ACTIVITIES
- Sideways slipping — as in Unit 1, Lesson 5
  (p. 102).
- Hopping wrestle — as in Unit 1, Lesson 5
  (p. 102).
- Partner cars — as in Unit 1, Lesson 4 (p. 102).
- Hand jump — as in Unit 1, Lesson 3 (p. 102).

GAMES
- Poison ball — use two balls.
- Boats — as in Unit 1, Lesson 2 (p. 101).
- Dog and cat — as in Unit 1, Lesson 2 (p. 101).
- Hit the tail — as in Unit 1, Lesson 5 (p. 102).

UNIT 2
GRADES 5~6
Gymnastics

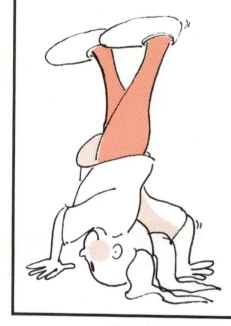

The children will experience running, rolling, jumping — trampet, tuck and straddle jump; balancing — headstand; weight on hands — vaulting horse.

Helpful hints

☐ Sequence work could be written on cards or on a blackboard for the children to see.

☐ Partner work is used extensively in this unit, so try and have each child with a different partner each day.

☐ Try and allow the less skilled child to feel that he/she has achieved in some small way.

☐ 'And long sit' still can be used as a means of getting the children's attention.

☐ Emphasize the care that needs to be taken when using large equipment.

☐ Are the children keen to demonstrate their skills?

RELATED CLASSROOM ACTIVITIES

Minor theme — our body

The muscular and skeletal systems — children look at the major muscle groups they use. Charts could be made to demonstrate the muscles and bones used in certain movements, e.g. bending and straightening the arm, bending and straightening the leg, throwing a ball, kicking a ball.

Muscle stretching — which muscles do we stretch before a certain activity? How does a VFL footballer warm up?

Minor theme — nutrition

Healthy breakfast, lunch and dinner. One meal could be discussed for a week, e.g. what is a healthy breakfast? Children could record for a certain time what they eat at various meals. These could then be analysed to see if the children are eating from the five main food groups. Have a breakfast at school for your grade. Children attempt to change a bad habit in their diet, e.g. eat fruit instead of potato chips at recess time.

Minor theme — leisure, games and fitness

What does fitness mean? Children should look at the different aspects of fitness, e.g. cardiovascular endurance, muscular endurance, strength and flexibility. Simple tests could be made for the children to test themselves now and at the end of the year.

What leisure activities are available to you in your community at the age you are now/when you are older? What is the difference between the type of leisure activities a young and old person would do?

Colonial games — a day could be spent playing games of our colonial days, e.g. kick the can, apple bobbing. Games peculiar to other countries could be looked at.

LESSON 1

Equipment
A small gym mat each.

Warm-up
Run and take off on one foot, land, run on.
Jump twisting the body in the air.
Jump and half twist/full twist to land on the same spot.

Skills
☐ Balancing — where whole of body weight is supported by partner, e.g. Partner A on four body supports, B on no body supports. Partner A on five body supports, B on no body supports. Partner A on two body supports, B on two body supports with feet as the highest part of balance.
☐ Revise backward roll — as in Unit 1, Lesson 5 (p. 91).
☐ Roll in one direction then a different direction.
☐ Twisting — two body parts moving the opposite way — children find different ways of twisting their body, e.g. from feet, twist body to face in different ways; on hands, twist body.

Application
☐ Perform the following sequence in groups of four: balance → roll any type → weight on hands activity → balance.

LESSON 2

Equipment
A cane between two, a small mat each.

Warm-up
Jump over cane held by partner — gradually increasing height.
Jump over cane with a half turn, a three-quarter turn, a full turn.

Skills
☐ Introduce headstand.
Ⓣ Children in pairs, one as support for the other: sit on heels, knees on mat and hands in line. Lean forward and place head on mat. Walk feet in until hips are high, slowly push feet upwards until legs are straight. Back slightly arched. Partner stands to the side to avoid being kicked.

☐ Partner balance with the cane as the highest part of the balance.
☐ Children make up their own balance with cane.
☐ Children practise any weight on hands activity over a cane.

Application
☐ Turning jump over cane → roll → weight on hands over cane → balance.

LESSON 3

Equipment
Trampet, large mats, cane.

Warm-up
Run quickly and stop suddenly. Change direction every time you stop.

Skills/Application
Perform the following two activities in two groups, rotating at half time.
1 Jumping with trampet (with teacher supervision).
Take off from one foot to land on trampet. Take off from two feet from trampet to land on floor. Jump up and not forward. Use arms to jump and balance.
☐ Jump, making various shapes in the air — wide, thin, curled.
☐ Jump, making a half/full turn in air.
☐ Jump over cane, gradually increase height.
2 Perform the following sequences in groups of four, each group on a large mat.
☐ Wide jump → wide roll.
☐ Jump half turn → backward roll.
☐ Jump half/full turn → weight on hands activity → balance.
Encourage children to find different ways of organizing their group — different starting positions and so on. Regularly stop grade to have

a look at the sequences that have been developed.

LESSON 4

Equipment
Trampet, gym mats, ten canes, beanbag each.

Warm-up
Run, throwing a beanbag into the air, jump to catch it.
Try various ways of moving your beanbag.

Skills
Perform the following two activities in two groups, rotating at half time.
1 Jumping on trampet with teacher supervision, introduce tuck jump.
(T) Bounce upwards and tuck heels up to bottom. Shoulders need to be level with hips to land balanced.

Introduce straddle jump — stretch legs out and lift as high as possible.
(D) 2 In groups of four, children devise their own sequence using a cane. It must include a jump, roll, weight on hands and balance.

LESSON 5

Equipment
Vaulting horse, springboard, a hoop each.

Warm-up
Each child with a hoop runs around area bowling hoop. Change speeds with direction from teacher.
Make various patterns, jumping in and out of hoop.
Jump over hoop while it is moving.

Skills

Perform the following two activities in two groups, rotating at half time.
1 On the vaulting horse with teacher supervision revise side-squat — bouncing hips up high, tuck knees close to stomach and place feet on horse.
☐ Introduce front vault

Place hands on horse sideways, jump upwards and lift hips high and legs over horse, land with both feet on opposite side. (T)
2 In groups of four, each group is given a particular sequence, e.g. group balance → roll away from each other → roll back to each other → group balance. Group balance → weight on hands activity → roll → group balance.

LESSON 6

Equipment
Vaulting horse, springboard, large mats, two long ropes, balance beam, trampet, twelve hoops, ten balls.

Warm-up
Leapfrog — groups of four make a line and leapfrog to line and back one after the other.

Skills/Application
☐ Gymnastics circuit — start children at different points and they rotate around equipment. Regularly stop circuit to demonstrate the different movements children are able to do. Try to get children to do something different from the person in front. Hoops and balls are placed at various activities. Teacher supervises the trampet.

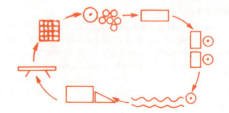

106

GRADES 5~6

Ball Handling

The children will experience kicking, pat bouncing, application games.

Helpful hints

- A quick way to get two teams is to let the children bob down with a partner, then one goes to Team A and the other to Team B.
- Letting children pick teams always leaves the less skilled child to be picked last which doesn't help his self-image.
- Colour bands are very useful to distinguish teams.
- Make sure you enjoy the lesson as well as the children.
- It is often rewarding to allow individual children to umpire a game or to take a lesson (prepared in advance).

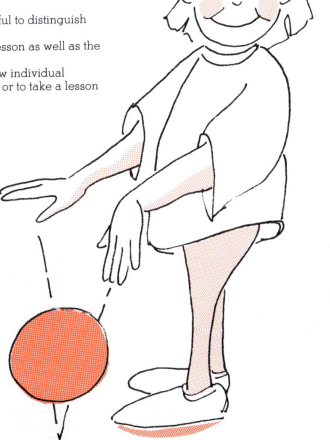

LESSON 1

Equipment
One ball between two, one block between two.

Warm-up
'Follow the leader' — the group jogs around a certain area, on signal the last person sprints to be leader, then the next person and so on.

Skills
(D)
- In pairs kick ball from the ground with right foot/left foot.
- Kick to the left of partner.
- Kick to the right of partner.
- Kick over various distances.
- Kick to hit a block. Children can do anything they like with block to improve their accuracy.

Application
- 'Kick chasey' — players in restricted area (e.g. netball court). Three to four players are selected as kickers, they kick a ball at the other players, trying to tag them below the knees with the ball. When tagged, players drop out. The game continues until all are tagged or allow a certain time limit.
- Relays — A kicks ball to B, B to C and so on, after kicking run to the end of the other line.

LESSON 2

Equipment
One ball between two, one block between two.

Warm-up
'Follow the leader' — as in Unit 2, Lesson 1, except instead of sprinting to the front the end person weaves in and out of the line to the front.

Skills
- In pairs, kick a dropped ball with right and left foot; to each side of partner.
- Start close together, each time your partner catches the ball, take one step out, if dropped, take one step in.
- Kick to hit a block — gradually increase distance.

Application
- Quick dodge the ball — divide the class into four teams and run two games concurrently. Team A in circular formation attempts to hit team B inside circle below the waist. When four of Team A are hit, teams immediately change over.
- Pat bouncing against team kicking — played by two teams. Each player in team A runs up to line and back pat bouncing a ball. Meanwhile team B kicks ball to each team member in turn. This continues until all of team A have finished. Swap over activities and see which team has the most kicks.

LESSON 3

Equipment
A ball each.

Warm-up
Tunnel ball.
Passing the ball over heads.
Passing the ball through legs and touching the ground.

Skills
- Pat bouncing — pat bounce ball with various body parts, e.g. hands, alternate hands, elbow, head and so on; at different points around body — side, behind, around; while walking, skipping, running, hopping; while balancing on one foot; while slowly sitting down and standing up; while looking ahead at a certain point.

Application
- Divide children into two groups, in circle formation. Two balls at opposite ends of circle. Pass balls around circle and on whistle, the children with the balls pat bounce their ball around the circle and back to their place, racing against each other.
- Relays — pat bounce ball up to line, back around team and pass to next person.

LESSON 4

Equipment
A ball each, a hoop each.

Warm-up

'Steal the balls' — number one from each team runs and collects a ball, pat bounces it back to his/her team's hoop. He/she tags number two who can collect a ball from centre hoop or some other team's hoop and pat bounce back to his/her hoop. Only one person from a team runs at any time, and only one ball can be picked up at a time.

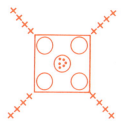

Skills

- ☐ Pat bounce ball inside hoop while standing outside.
- ☐ Pat bounce ball outside hoop, while standing inside hoop.
- ☐ In pairs, A bounces ball inside the hoop and B tries to take the ball away (your body should be between the ball and your partner).
- Ⓓ ☐ See if partners can create a new game using a ball and a hoop.

Application

- ☐ Standing in a large circle, with two balls, two children next to each other start with the ball and pat bounce it to every second person, until the balls reach their leaders. First ball back is the winner.

- ☐ Pat bouncing against team kicking — as in Unit 2, Lesson 2 (p. 108).

LESSON 5

Equipment

Two cricket stumps, four balls, rounders court (or area marked by four hoops).

Warm-up

'Tunnel ball' — passing the ball overhead; passing the ball through legs without touching ground; passing ball alternately overhead and through legs.

Skills/Application

- ☐ Target ball — two even groups, two games. Each group stands in circle formation, with two balls and a cricket stump in the centre. The stump is guarded by a player who uses hands or feet to deflect or stop balls that are kicked at the tower by the circle players. Any player who hits the stumps changes places with the defender.
- ☐ Kick ball rounders — two even teams, rounders court. Team A, one at a time, kicks the ball from bowler and attempts to complete a circuit of the court while the fielders make five to eight (depending on the ability) passes with the ball. A point is scored if the kicker can complete a rounder. Swap over after three kickers fail to make a circuit.

LESSON 6

Equipment

One ball, rounders court (or four hoops).

Warm-up

'One versus three' — groups of four, numbers one to three, join hands to make a triangle. A fourth person tries to touch the number three person in the triangle. When successful he/she changes places with number three and the game starts again.

Skills/Application

- ☐ Extended tunnel ball — two even teams, one fielding, one kicking. The kicking team kicks the ball and runs around the four bases before the fielders tunnel the ball through each others' legs. The last fielder calls 'stop' when the ball reaches him/her. A run is scored if the kicker reaches home before 'stop' is called. When three kickers don't make home, teams swap over.

This number can be changed, depending on the Ⓣ ability of the children, but it is best to keep teams swapping over regularly to prevent children getting bored in kicking line.

GRADES 5~6
Major Games

The children will experience the following skills of soccer: trapping, kicking, dribbling, tackling.

Helpful hints

- In a game situation rotate major positions so all children have a turn. This can be done by giving children a number and taking it in turns.
- Allow children time to practise the skill if they are giving a demonstration.
- Try and watch every child in a phys. ed. lesson at least every second lesson, but ideally every lesson.
- Make sure balls are pumped up before the start of the lesson.
- Are the children active and energetic?

LESSON 1

Equipment
A soccer ball (or similar) between two.

Warm-up
'Numbers relay' — class is divided into two long files sitting on the ground opposite each other with legs out straight. Players are numbered from the front down. The teacher calls out a number, this person runs over the legs to the front, down the side of team and up the centre over legs back to position. First back wins a point for the team. Two numbers can be called at once.

Skills
- Trapping — in pairs roll the ball to each other and try to stop it 'dead'.

Ⓣ Demonstrate using sole of the foot — push the sole of foot down on ball to stop bounce; eyes on ball, head down, slightly leaning forward. Practise this technique.

Ⓓ Demonstrate inside foot trap — turn leg sideways and lean over ball; the inside of foot moves down on ball.
  - Partners roll ball and trap either way ten times each.
  - Roll ball to either side of partner.

Application
- Soccer dodge ball — divide the class into four teams and have two games running concurrently. Team X, by passing and trapping ball with feet, attempts to hit member of team O below the waist. When four of the team have been hit, change over teams.

LESSON 2

Equipment
One soccer ball between two, one block between two.

Warm-up
'Follow the leader' — the group jogs around a certain area, on signal the last person sprints to be leader, then the next person and so on.

Skills
- Kicking — low straight kick.

Non-kicking foot is placed beside the ball, the other foot is swung backwards. Eyes on ball, point toes forward, laces of shoe hit the ball. Ⓣ
- In pairs, drop ball, allow to bounce and kick to partner; kick at a block to hit it.
- Inside foot pass.

Foot is kept at right angles, the whole foot is used; a quick push is made, follow foot through low. Ⓣ
- Outside foot pass — as above except use the outside of the foot. Practise the above passes.

Application
- Block ball — divide the class into groups of six to seven, three to four balls per group, five blocks. Each team tries to knock down the blocks by kicking the ball at them. If the ball lands between the two lines it can be retrieved but not kicked until back at the line. The team that knocks over the most blocks wins.
- Cross ball — in groups of six to seven, instead of throwing, children pass the ball with feet to each other.

LESSON 3

Equipment
One soccer ball between two, sixteen blocks, twenty beanbags, five hoops.

Warm-up
'Steal the beanbags' — as in Unit 2, Lesson 4 — Ball handling (p. 109) except beanbags are used instead of balls.

Skills
- Dribbling — tap or push the ball with the inside or outside of the foot.

Body slightly forward, eyes on ball, the ball is kept very close to the feet. Ⓣ
- With a partner, dribble the ball around your partner keeping it close to your body.
- Dribble ball and when partner claps, change direction quickly.
- Partner leads the way and you follow dribbling ball.

111

Application

- Obstacle relay — groups of six to eight dribble ball in and out of blocks.
- Steal the soccer balls — as above, in warm-up, except use soccer balls instead of beanbags and dribble the ball back to your hoop. Begin with two balls in each hoop and five in the centre hoop.
- Block ball — as in Unit 2, Lesson 2 (p. 111).

LESSON 4

Equipment
One soccer ball between two.

Warm-up
'Partner races' — A dribbles ball to line and back, B once tagged, repeats. First pair back are the winners. A dribbles to line, dribbles back half way and kicks ball to B, who repeats. In pairs, five metres apart, ten quick passes each.

Skills
- Tackling opponent to get the ball.
- ⓣ Try and get one foot to make contact with ball; it is best to tackle when the ball is furthest from, or just out of control of, partner.
- In pairs, A tries to prevent B from dribbling the ball from one line to the next.
- Groups of four — number one, two and three pass or dribble the ball while number four tries to touch it. Change players around. Then change to two players against two players for 'keeping off'.

Application
- Kick a goal — number off two teams, as in diagram. Teacher calls a number, those children attempt to get the ball through their goals. You can call two or three numbers at a time.

```
  1 2 3 4 5 6 7 8 9 10
- × × × × × × × × × × -
           •
- × × × × × × × × × × -
 10 9 8 7 6 5 4 3 2 1
```

LESSON 5

Equipment
Two soccer balls, three blocks.

Warm-up
'Numbers relay' — as in Unit 2, Lesson 1 (p. 111).

Skills/Application

- Rounder soccer — divide class into two teams, one kicking, one fielding. Bowler throws ball underarm to kicker who kicks into the area. He/she then dribbles another ball around a block and back as many times as possible. The fielding team can stop the ball using no hands and the ball must be passed, using feet, by three fielders then shoot for goal. Once the ball goes through the goals the batter stops and his/her score is the number of times he/she dribbles the ball up to the line and back. Teams swap over after five kicks, rotate positions of bowler.

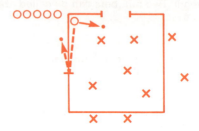

LESSON 6

Equipment
One soccer ball, four blocks.

Warm-up
'One, two, three' — two lines face each other, netball court width apart. Three extra players stand in the centre. The centre and line players number off in threes. When teacher calls 'threes' the threes change sides and the centre three tries to catch as many as he/she can. Tagged players stay in the centre and help catch their number.

Skills/Application

- Simplified soccer — each team divides evenly in the three areas of the netball court. The ball must be passed in each area before a goal can be scored. Players must stay in their own area. Rotate areas every five minutes. The game is started with a bounced ball in the centre.

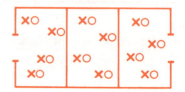

GRADES 5~6
Minor Games/Fitness

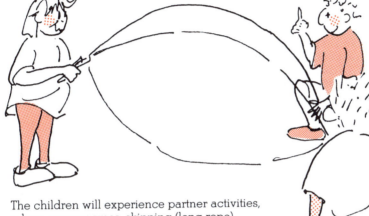

The children will experience partner activities, relays, group games, skipping (long rope), running.

Helpful hints
- Reinforce the boundaries for various games.
- Remind children to always look where they are running.
- Encourage the children to be honest in game situations.
- Ensure that all children have a turn at being 'he'. For the slower children, two 'hes' can be selected together to keep the game exciting.
- Make sure the children are kept active and energetic.
- Are the children able to play cooperatively in groups?

LESSON 1

Equipment
Two balls, twelve beanbags.

Warm-up
Running — jog on the spot, holding hands at waist level and bring knees up to touch hands. Run making ground patterns such as circles, squares, zig-zags. Run following the pattern of a partner.

PARTNER ACTIVITIES
- Circle run — partner A holds hand up, while B runs around him/her and hits the hand as he/she passes. After five times, partners change places.
- Touch hands — partners stand back to back, bend over and touch hands between their legs and then above their head.
- Knee chasey — partner A is chased by B until B can touch A behind the knee. Roles are changed every thirty seconds. Stay in small areas.

- Monkey grip — use a monkey grip and work arms backwards and forwards as quickly as you can.

GAMES
- Chase the beanbag — twelve children hold a beanbag. Three children are 'he' and try to tag a player in possession of a beanbag. If successful a new chaser is chosen. Children run and dodge and pass on the beanbag if close to getting caught.
- Poison ball — use two balls.
- Dog and cat — as in Unit 1, Lesson 2 — Minor games/fitness (p. 101).
- Train chasey — children in pairs with one player left. Each player forms a train, the front the engine, the back the carriage. The odd player tries to attach himself/herself to the back of one of the trains. If successful the engine of that train drops off and attaches himself/herself to another train and so on.

LESSON 2

Equipment
Four balls.

Warm-up
'Crumbs and crusts' — children face each other in two lines, one metre apart, one is 'crumbs' and the other 'crusts'. The teacher calls 'crumbs' or 'crusts' and the line called runs away, chased by the other line. If caught, join that line.

PARTNER ACTIVITIES
- Leapfrog — children leapfrog over each other to line and back.
- Knee chasey — as in Unit 2, Lesson 1.
- Monkey grip — as in Unit 2, Lesson 1.
- Arm strength — with elbows up and hands together, partner tries to separate opponent's arms.

RELAYS
- Piggy back — teams divide up into pairs who piggy back one at a time up to line and back.
- Trains — as in Unit 1, Lesson 1 — Minor games/fitness.
- Carry your toes — holding toes, hop up to line and sprint back.
- Cross over relays — number 1 from each team runs around opposite team, tags number 2 and so on.
- Repeat above, except a ball is dribbled around the opposite team and back.

- Repeat above, except number 1 passes ball overhead to number 2 and down the line. The end person sprints around the opposite team and back to the start of the team. The ball is then passed overhead as before.

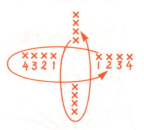

LESSON 3

Equipment
Long skipping rope, one ball.

Warm-up
'Hopping chasey' — players hop while chasing each other. Have four children as 'he'. Change chasers regularly.

PARTNER ACTIVITIES
- Hopping bumps — partners hold up one leg and place their other hand behind their back. They then bump each other until one places the other foot on the ground.
- Leapfrog — as in Unit 2, Lesson 2.
- Arm strength — as in Unit 2, Lesson 2.
- Partner standing — partners sit back to back with knees bent and arms interlocked. Try and stand up together whilst backs remain together. Go from sitting to standing, and vice-versa.

SKIPPING
- Run through long rope one after the other; then miss one loop, then no misses.
- Run through with partners — miss one, no misses.
- Run in, jump one and then out — miss one, no misses.
- As above with partner.
- Have a competition to see who can stay in for the longest.

GAMES
- Hit the tail — children stand in circle with five in the centre, holding onto waists. Children on outside of circle throw ball to hit the last person in line until there is only one left. The front person can only hit or kick the ball, but if caught on the full is also out.

LESSON 4

Equipment
A long skipping rope.

Warm-up
'Fight the bombers' — as in Unit 1, Lesson 2 — Minor games/fitness (p. 101).

PARTNER ACTIVITIES
- Partner cars — partners face each other with hands on shoulders. Partner A moves backwards while B steers. On signal, reverse direction.
- Hopping bumps — as in Unit 2, Lesson 3 (p. 114).
- Partner standing — as in Unit 2, Lesson 3
- Wheelbarrow races.

SKIPPING
- Revise skipping with a long rope as in Unit 2, Lesson 3.

GAMES
- Square chase — four teams arranged in a square. Each team member is given a number and when called races around the square and back to place.

- Boats — in groups of four, players form a file with hands on hips of person in front. On a signal the team hops on right legs to line and then reverse order and direction to hop back to starting line on left legs.

LESSON 5

Equipment
Two balls, long skipping rope.

Warm-up
'Hunters and hares' — two children are the hunters and have a ball each. The rest line up, being the hares. Each hunter in turn decides how the hares will move to the next line, e.g. run, hop, walk, crawl, etc. The two hunters perform the same movement and attempt to hit the hares with the balls. When hit, the hares remain where they were hit and become poisonous trees. This means they can reach out their hands and tag any hares that come near their tree. Each time the hares make it safely to the end of line a new movement is called.

Distance run — children run around school as many times as they can within a ten minute time limit.

SKIPPING
- Repeat Unit 2, Lesson 3.
- Introduce alphabet skip — one person at a time jumps in for one and then out with the following rhyme.
  1st...A
  2nd... word that begins with A, e.g. apple
  3rd...B
  4th... word that begins with B, e.g. banana.

GAME
- Poison ball — use two balls.

LESSON 6

Equipment
Long skipping rope, ball, twelve beanbags.

Warm-up
Distance run — children see how far they can run in ten minutes, e.g. laps of the school, oval, etc.

SKIPPING
- Revise alphabet skip as in Unit 2, Lesson 5.
- Skip to any rhymes that children know.

GAMES
- Train chasey — as in Unit 2, Lesson 1 (p. 114).
- Chase the beanbag — as in Unit 2, Lesson 1 (p. 114).
- Hit the tail — as in Unit 2, Lesson 3 (p. 115).
- Square chasey — as in Unit 2, Lesson 4 (p. 115).
- Boats — as in Unit 2, Lesson 4 (p. 115).

GRADES 5~6

Gymnastics

The children will experience jumping, rolling, balance, balance beam, weight on hands, vaulting horse — through vault, forward roll.

Helpful hints

- ☐ Make sure children are aware of the safety aspects of the equipment being used.
- ☐ Do not force all children to do a certain vault, but give them something to aim for, rather than doing nothing.
- ☐ Use of two groups rotating is made in this unit, so pay regular attention to the group working on their own.
- ☐ When giving a demonstration in gymnastics, make sure it shows the correct technique.
- ☐ Make sure that you enjoy the lesson as well as the children.
- ☐ Are the children willing to try new challenges?
- ☐ Videotaping the sequences is a great tool for motivation.

RELATED CLASSROOM ACTIVITIES

Minor theme — our body

Body parts — children look at various parts of the body and discover their function. Groups of children could be given different body parts to work on, e.g. eyes, brain, heart, lungs, kidneys, small and large intestines and so on.

Minor theme — nutrition

Diet — children should be aware of the various diets, e.g. crash diets as seen in many magazines, special diets for people with high cholesterol problems, etc. The problems of crash diets can be discussed. Do you really lose weight in the long run? What is anorexia? Do we eat too much salt and sugar? How much salt is in tinned food as compared with fresh food? What type of food do you eat in between meals?

Minor theme — leisure, games and fitness

☐ Smoking — a unit could be developed on the effects of smoking in basic terms. Group discussion/projects could reflect on why children and adults smoke.

☐ The Olympic Games — the history of Australia in the games. The different types of events — these could be grouped in various ways, e.g. team/individual, contact/non-contact. Types of skills used, e.g. throwing, hitting and so on.

☐ Games the children play can be analysed to discover which skills are involved.

LESSON 1

Equipment

A small rope each, balance beam, ten balls, beanbag, hoops, canes.

Warm-up

Each child has a small rope and moves with the rope on the spot and travelling.

Skills

☐ Weight on hands — introduce 'round-off'.

This is very similar to a cartwheel, except legs meet at the highest point. As the legs meet, the hips make a half turn. Feet and legs snap down.

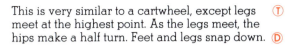

Application

Two groups can rotate around the following activities.

1. Balance beam (with teacher supervision) — introduce safety features: when on beam, concentrate and do not look at other children. Experiment with different ways of walking across beam, encourage each child to do something different, e.g. forwards, backwards, sideways — heel to toe, right foot always in front of left and vice-versa, balancing beanbag, bouncing ball.

2. Weight on hands — partners practise round-off (one as spotter).

☐ Sequence with partner, using equipment — ball, hoop, beanbag or cane. Any type of jump → weight on hands → any type of roll.

LESSON 2

Equipment

Springboard, vaulting horse, balance beam, large mat, two hoops and balls.

Warm-up

'One versus three' — in groups of four, numbers one and two join hands. A fourth person tries to touch number three in the group. When successful, change places with the number three and start again.

Skills

☐ In groups of three, children stand arms distance apart, while the third child runs up, places his/her hands on each shoulder, lifts legs and hips up high and jumps through. Swap over positions.

Application

☐ Two groups can rotate around:

1. Vaulting activities using springboard,

117

vaulting horse, large mat.

- ☐ Revise front vault — as in Unit 2, Lesson 5 (p. 106).

Ⓣ Emphasize lifting hips up high, increase height of horse.

- ☐ Introduce through vault.

Ⓣ Two children sit on horse with arms supporting weight on horse. Children run up, jump on springboard, place hands on shoulders and bring feet through to land on horse. Repeat, except go right over horse.

2 Experiment with the following balance sequence: walking to centre of beam in various ways → stationary balance → different ways of moving to end of beam.

LESSON 3

Equipment
Vaulting horse, springboard, large mat, five balls, canes and hoops.

Warm-up
Groups of four to five children in a line, leapfrog over each other one at a time, up to line and back.

Skills/Application
Two groups can rotate around the following activities.

1 Through vault (with teacher supervision) — as children gain confidence let them try to through vault without children sitting on the horse.

Children begin by placing their feet on the horse. Gradually get the hands to the far end and bring the feet all the way over. Teacher spots in front and takes the upper arms of the children. Ⓣ

2 In groups of four, children work out to the following sequence using balls, hoops or canes — any balance → roll → balance. Balance → weight on hands → balance.

LESSON 4

Equipment
Vaulting horse, springboard, large mat, five balls, hoops and canes.

Warm-up
Relays — tunnel ball, ball over head and under legs.

Skills/Application
1 Vaulting (with teacher supervision).

- ☐ Introduce forward roll over the horse lengthways.

Get hips up high, tuck head under, with weight Ⓣ on hands. Lower shoulders and roll. Legs are not tucked tightly

- ☐ Vault to box, stop and then forward roll.
- ☐ Vault to box and forward roll along.
- ☐ Revise through vault — as in Unit 3, Lesson 3.

2 Groups of four develop sequence from Unit 3, Lesson 3 by adding another section, i.e. balance → weight on hands → roll → balance. Children use various types of equipment.

LESSON 5

Equipment
Springboard, vaulting horse, large mats, two

ropes, balance beam, trampet, twelve balls, hoops and canes.

Warm-up
'One versus three' — as in Unit 3, Lesson 3 (p. 117).

Skills/Application
▫ Gymnastics circuit — children spread out evenly and rotate around equipment, having a turn at each piece of equipment.

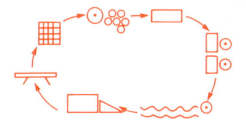

Encourage a variety of ideas. Stop the class regularly to demonstrate different ideas. Ⓣ

LESSON 6

Equipment
As in Unit 3, Lesson 5.

Warm-up
'Leapfrog' — as in Unit 3, Lesson 3 (p. 118).

Skills/Application
▫ Gymnastics — as in Unit 3, Lesson 5.
Variation: 'follow the leader' — children rotate around the circuit with a partner.

GRADES 5~6

Ball Handling

The children will experience dribbling; hitting — bats, hockey sticks; application games.

Helpful hints

- ☐ A quick way to get two teams is to let the children bob down with a partner, then one goes to team A and the other to team B.
- ☐ Letting children pick teams always leaves the less skilled child last to be picked, which does not help the self-confidence.
- ☐ In a major game situation, rotate major positions by giving all children a number and taking it in turns.
- ☐ In hot weather especially, time should be allowed at the end of a lesson for a quick drink as children dehydrate very quickly.
- ☐ Make sure you enjoy the lesson as well as the children.

LESSON 1

Equipment
A ball each (tennis or bounce).

Warm-up
'Fight the bombers'.

Skills

- ☐ Bounce ball three times and hit with head.
- ☐ Bounce ball three times, hit with head and then catch.
- ☐ Dribble ball while standing still/moving.
- ☐ Dribble ball while looking up at a certain object.
- ☐ Dribble ball around body.

- In pairs, stand back to back and dribble ball around each other.
- Dribble ball around partner and swap over.
- Holding inside hands, alternately bounce ball — while standing still, walking, skipping, jogging.

Application
- Dribbling race — two equal teams, children numbered from opposite ends. Teacher calls a number and those two children run out to the centre, pick up the ball and dribble it back over their team's line. If ball is taken over by person without being tagged by partner (with ball in possession) a point is scored.
  Variation: call two numbers at a time and children work as a team.

LESSON 2

Equipment
One ball between two, six chairs, four blocks, two canes and two long ropes.

Warm-up
'Hunters and hares'.

Skills
- With a partner, holding inside hands, alternately bounce ball.
- As above, except have races the length of the netball court.
- Piggy back each other with the top person bouncing the ball/alternately bouncing ball with partner.
- In groups of three, two against one — 'keepings off' — two people dribble the ball,

the other attempts to touch the ball and then swaps positions.
- One against two — as above — change positions regularly.

Application
- Move freely around obstacle course using the equipment listed above. Stop children to give various demonstrations and ideas with equipment, e.g. climb over chairs and pat bounce, sit on chairs and pat bounce, crawl under cane and pat bounce, jump over cane and pat bounce.
- Working in pairs one person follows the other's instructions.
- Dribbling race — as in Unit 3, Lesson 1.

LESSON 3

Equipment
A bat each (bat tennis or rounders), a tennis ball each.

Warm-up
'Skipping chase' — groups of five to six children skip in a confined area while the chaser, who also skips, attempts to tag them.

Skills
- Continuously hit ball into the air using your hand.
- Continuously hit ball into the air using a bat.
- Hit ball, let it bounce, hit ball, bounce, etc.
- Bounce twice, hit two to five times, etc.
- Hit ball at various heights.
- Stand up and sit down while hitting ball.
- In pairs, one bat and ball between two, A passes ball to B in any way so that he/she can hit it back, e.g. bounce and hit, throw and hit, roll and hit, throw high and hit. Swap activities with partner.
- Children join inside hands and alternately hit ball — on the spot, while walking.

Application
- Hitting against team running — divide class into two teams. Each player in team A runs around the netball court (or similar distance). Team B stands in a circle, each with a bat and one person in the centre who hits the ball to each person in the circle, counting the number of hits they get in the time it takes all of team A to complete their run. Swap activities.

LESSON 4

Equipment
A hockey stick each, a tennis ball between two, one block each.

Warm-up
'Leapfrog chasey' — when tagged you remain in a crouch position, until someone leapfrogs over you.

Skills
- In pairs, hit ball along ground to each other using hockey sticks.
- Try and hit through two blocks to partner.
- Gradually decrease the distance between the blocks as the skill increases and also increase the distance from the blocks.

Application
- In groups of six to eight, number six hits the ball to number one and so on to number five who runs out and takes number six's position and continues the pattern. Number six goes to number one's position and everyone else moves up one place.
- Circle hockey — children in circle formation, two balls at opposite ends of circle, and two hockey sticks in centre. Pass ball around circle and on whistle, the two holding a ball, run to the centre, get a hockey stick and dribble their ball around the circle and back to their place, racing against the other person.

LESSON 5

Equipment
A hockey stick each, one ball between three.

Warm-up
'Fight the bombers'.

Skills
- In groups of three, number one rolls back to number two who hits ball to number three

and then back to number one. Rotate positions.
- As above, but number two tries to hit the ball through number one's legs to number three and then back to number one. Rotate positions after five hits.

Application
- Hockey race — two equal teams numbered from opposite ends. Teacher calls a number and those two players run out to centre, pick up a hockey stick and try to dribble the ball over their team's line. Variation: call two, three or four numbers at a time.

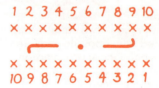

- Relays — dribble ball up to line and back, hit ball to team-mate and run to end of line.

LESSON 6

Equipment
Rounders diamond or similar area marked by five hoops, rounders bat, tennis ball.

Warm-up
'Leapfrog chasey' — as in Unit 3, Lesson 4.

Skills/Application
- Bowler rounders — divide class into two teams, one batting, one fielding. Bowler throws underarm to batter, when the ball is hit the batter must run to the bases. The fielders return the ball to the bowler. Any base-runners who are between the bases when the bowler has the ball, are out. A batter can be caught out. Three out 'side away'. A runner may pass another. There may be more than one runner on a base. The batter must hit the ball, don't count the strikes. The teacher can bowl for both teams.

UNIT 3

GRADES 5~6
Major Games

The children will experience the following skills of cricket: throwing, catching, fielding, bowling, batting.

Helpful hints
- ☐ Let the children know that cricket is not only a male sport, girls should be just as keen.
- ☐ Have demonstrations ready in advance.
- ☐ Use different children for demonstrations.
- ☐ Keep children on the move all the time, this prevents boredom and discipline problems.
- ☐ Reward and encourage triers.
- ☐ Reinforce teaching skills in the classroom before going outside.
- ☐ Teacher interest and involvement have a very positive effect on the lesson.

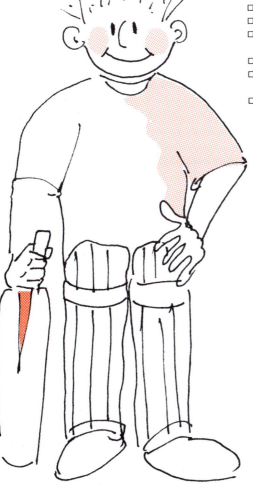

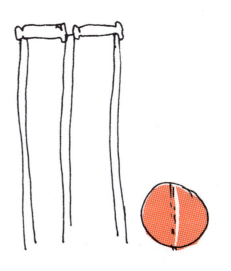

LESSON 1

Equipment
Four large balls, a tennis ball each, four sets of cricket stumps.

Warm-up
'Cross relay' — one ball each team. Number one runs around circle with ball and back to his/her team to take number five's position. He/she passes the ball down the line to number two who then repeats the process.

```
                    × 1
                    × 2
                    × 3
                    × 4
    1 2 3 4 5 × 5
    × × × × ×   × × × × ×
              5 × 5 4 3 2 1
              4 ×
              3 ×
              2 ×
              1 ×
```

Skills
- Each person with a ball throws it in the air and catches it — standing still/moving to catch it.
- Partners give high catches to each other.
- Run to field a ball on the first bounce and throw back to partner.
- (T) When fielding, make sure body is behind ball.
- Throw short quick throws to each other over a short distance (approx. one metre).

Application
- Roll, run and throw relay — number one rolls ball to line, runs to collect it and throws it back to number two, and so on.

```
    × × × × ×
    5 4 3 2 1
```

- Hit the stumps relay — number one throws ball underarm/overarm at cricket stumps while number six retrieves and throws ball to number two. Number one runs to retrieve next shot. Count the number of successful hits.

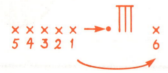

LESSON 2

Equipment
A tennis ball each, four sets of cricket stumps, one cricket bat.

Warm-up
'Hit the stumps relay' — as in Unit 3, Lesson 1.

Skills
- Standing target throw — wicket stumps are placed against the wall. Each child one at a time aims to hit the stumps, fields the ball and goes to the end of the line.
- As above, except after throwing, run to touch stumps and then chase ball.

- In pairs, A throws at wall, while B aims to catch the ball on the full. Gradually increase difficulty.

Application
- Keep the ball off the ground — played in groups of eight, rotating two pairs on bat-tennis court with two pairs off the court. Players throw the ball back and forth trying to get the opposition to drop the ball. The team that drops the ball or misses it, rotates off and the nest team comes on. The ball can only be thrown at knee height and below.
- Running between wickets against hitting the stumps — team A, one at a time runs to wickets and back as quickly as possible, holding a bat. Team B — throw ball at cricket stump one at a time and count the successful throws in the time it takes team A to finish its run. Teams swap over to see who can hit the stumps the most number of times.

LESSON 3

Equipment
One tennis ball between two, cricket bat, two cricket stumps.

124

Warm-up

'Running between wickets against catching' — as in Unit 3, Lesson 2, except Team B see how many catches they can get in the time limit.

Skills

- Bowling

(T) Grip ball in fingers, not in palm of hand, two fingers either side of the seam and thumb underneath. Body side on, feet apart, weight on back foot. Unwind arms — fully stretched, over and past the ear. Front foot steps forward just before arm comes past the ear. Have front shoulder and elbow pointing at wickets. Demonstrate the correct basic action.

- In pairs, practise bowling action to each other and check each other's action.
- Gradually introduce a run-up.

Application

- Catching and fielding against bowling at stumps — two groups perform the two activities and then swap over.
1 Try to get as many catches as possible in a circle formation.

2 Number 1 bowls to hit stumps, number 2 retrieves, throws to number 3 who continues. Number 1 runs to stumps to retrieve next ball. Lines rotate until a total of 10 successful bowls have been completed, then stop.
   Teams swap and the number of catches are compared.

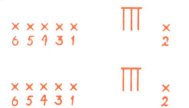

LESSON 4

Equipment

One tennis ball between two, one cricket bat between two, four cricket stumps.

Warm-up

'Cross relay' — as in Unit 3, Lesson 1 (p. 124).

Skills

- Batting and bowling — introduce the basic skill of batting — forward defence.

Grip — bat flat on ground, place both hands (T) over the top and pick up bat, not twisting handle. Stance — feet slightly apart, toes in line, bat close to rear toe. Weight on both feet. Top hand controls the shots. Keep elbow up. Front foot placed almost in line with ball.

- In pairs, A bowls to B who practises the basic forward defence.

Application

- Batting relay — divide the class into four teams. Number one rolls ball to B who hits back, number one fields and gives it to number two and runs behind number five. When all five players have rolled ball, number one becomes batter and B becomes number five.

- Batting groups — divide the class into four teams. One player is the batter, the others in the team, the fielders. One fielder rolls ball to batter who hits it back. Whoever fields, rolls the ball. After five hits change batters.

- Hit below the knees — also played in four teams. Fielders aim to hit the batter below the knees with the ball. The batter uses his/her bat to stop the ball. Fielders throw ball from where they field it. The batter can also be caught out.

LESSON 5

Equipment

One cricket bat between two, one tennis ball between two.

Warm-up

'Cricket dribble' — played in pairs with a bat and ball. Partner A dribbles ball around netball courts or designated area, then B does the same. Variations: walking, running sideways.

Skills

☐ Batting — introduce forward straight drive.

Ⓣ Front foot steps forward to line of ball. Bat is brought forward, close to pad, with elbow up. Follow through, keeping bat straight.

☐ In pairs, throw ball from a short distance and partner practises shot.

Application

☐ Batting groups — as in Unit 3, Lesson 4.
☐ Batting relay — as in Unit 3, Lesson 4.
☐ Hit below the knees — as in Unit 3, Lesson 4.

LESSON 6

Equipment

One tennis ball between two, three cricket stumps, three cricket bats, six blocks.

Warm-up

'Name ball' — played in groups of approximately four, with a leader in the middle of circle who throws up ball, calls out name or number of another player who runs forward to take the catch on the full. Return ball to leader.

Skills/Application

☐ Tabloids — children in pairs rotate around four activity stations, scoring for each other. A performs activity while B counts. Spend five minutes at each activity (two minutes each person).

Activity 1 — throwing and catching — see how many catches are made.

Activity 2 — bowling — use proper action, see how many times the wickets are hit.

Activity 3 — batting. Standing approximately six metres apart, partner A bowls to B and counts how many hits go back to the bowler's line.

Activity 4 — throwing for accuracy. See how many times one block can be hit from six to ten metres away. Partner resets blocks.

GRADES 5~6
Minor Games/Fitness

The children will experience partner activities, relays, medicine ball activities, hopscotch, skipping.

Helpful hints
- Keep the children active for the whole lesson.
- Encourage the children to help each other; accept all children regardless of their abilities.
- Take advantage of any child's creativity, especially with hopscotch and skipping.
- In hot weather especially, make time at the end of a lesson for a quick drink.
- Reward and encourage triers.
- Teacher interest and involvement has a very positive effect on the outcome of the lesson.

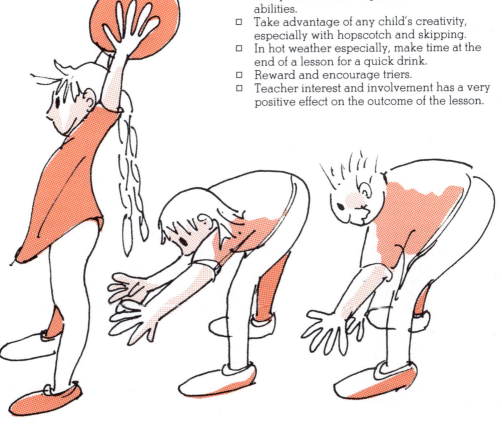

LESSON 1

Equipment
A long skipping rope.

Warm-up
'Leapfrog relay' — in groups of four to five, children leapfrog over each other to the line and back.

Skills/Application
RELAYS
- Partner relay — each team is divided into pairs who run to line and back. Variations: running side to side, running holding onto waists, moving with ankles touching.
- Through the legs — all players standing astride. The end person crawls through legs of team to front, runs up to line and tags the next player and so on.

SKIPPING
- Revision of Unit 2 activities (p. 115).
- Individuals — running through, miss one loop, miss no loops, with jumps.
- Partners run through as above.
- Introduce various rhymes for the children to chant while skipping. The children will be able to suggest many.

LESSON 2

Equipment
Counters (markers for hopscotch).

Warm-up
'Fight the bombers'.

Skills/Application
PARTNER ACTIVITIES
- Partner run — on go, A runs to line and returns to touch B's hand. B then runs to line and back to A. See how many times partners' hands touch in one minute.
- Touch hands — standing back to back, partners bend and touch hands between legs and then above head.
- Hopping bumps — partners hold up one leg and place their other hand behind back. They then bump each other until one places the other foot on the ground.

HOPSCOTCH
- Introduce/revise normal hopscotch rules.

10	9 11	10
6	5 7	6
2	1 3	2

4, 8, 12

- Introduce 'square hopscotch' — hop in middle square of first row, one foot in two outside squares. Hop into middle square. Hop out. The above is repeated in the second and third lines. This game can also be played backwards.
- Children in groups of four to six, play their own game of 'square' or normal hopscotch. Children rotate between the two games.

LESSON 3

Equipment
Four bounce balls, long skipping rope, counters.

Warm-up
Run around school block/school once or twice.

Skills/Application
RELAYS
- Tunnel ball — played by four teams.
- Over the legs — played by four teams, sitting with legs out straight. Number one runs up to line behind his/her team and jumps over the legs, back to starting position. Number two jumps over number one, runs up the line, behind team and over legs back to starting position and so on.

HOPSCOTCH
As in Unit 3, Lesson 2

SKIPPING
As in Unit 3, Lesson 1. Children rotate between hopscotch and skipping.

LESSON 4

Equipment
Four balls, counters, long skipping rope.

Warm-up

'Hunters and hares' — two hunters, each with a ball, try to hit the hares, who stand as poisoned trees if hit.

Skills/Application
PARTNER ACTIVITIES
- Partner run — as in Unit 3, Lesson 2 (p. 128).
- Hopping bumps — as in Unit 3, Lesson 2 (p. 128).

RELAYS
- Tunnel ball.
- Pass the ball over the head.
- Pass the ball through the legs.

HOPSCOTCH/SKIPPING
Children rotate between the two activities.

LESSON 5

Equipment
Medicine balls and large balls between two, two long skipping ropes.

Warm-up
'Hopping chasey' — players hop while chasing each other. Have four children as 'he', change regularly.

Skills/Application
PARTNER ACTIVITIES
- Hop, carrying the ball with one knee and forehead.

- Crabwalk with the ball between the knees.

- Ball between knees — races.

- Throw ball up with feet to catch in the hands.
- Throw ball with feet to catch in the hands.
- Sit-ups with the arms out straight. Take ball behind the head.

GAMES
- Hit the tail — as in Unit 2, Lesson 3 — Minor games (p. 115)

SKIPPING
- Turning two large ropes at once, play French ropes — turn in, and Dutch ropes — turn out.

LESSON 6

Equipment
One medicine ball or other large ball between two, or small rope each, two large skipping ropes.

Warm-up
'Leapfrog relay' — as in Unit 3, Lesson 1 (p. 128).

Skills/Application
As in Unit 3, Lesson 5.

SKIPPING
- With small ropes, skip forwards, backwards, while moving sideways, hopping on one foot, cross arms on every alternate step.
- In pairs, partner A holding rope, B Skipping with him/her. Partners holding inner hands, skip together.
- Revise French ropes and Dutch ropes, as in Unit 3, Lesson 5.

GAME
- Poison ball — using two balls.

Notes

Notes

Notes

Notes